Death & Life

15 The Chambers, Vineyard
Abingdon OX14 3FE
brf.org.uk

Bible Reading Fellowship is a charity (233280)
and company limited by guarantee (301324),
registered in England and Wales

ISBN 978 1 80039 283 0
First published 2024
10 9 8 7 6 5 4 3 2 1 0
All rights reserved

Text © Joanna Collicutt, Jo Ind, Victoria Slater and Alison Webster 2024
This edition © Bible Reading Fellowship 20224
Cover image © Diana Darkmoon/stock.adobe.com

The authors assert the moral right to be identified as the authors of this work

Acknowledgements
Unless otherwise stated, scripture quotations are taken from New Revised Standard Version Updated Edition. Copyright © 2021 National Council of Churches of Christ in the United States of America. Used by permission. All rights reserved worldwide. Scripture quotations marked NIV are taken from The Holy Bible, New International Version® Anglicized, NIV® Copyright © 1979, 1984, 2011 by Biblica, Inc.® Used by permission. All rights reserved worldwide.

Scripture quotations marked NIV are taken from The Holy Bible, New International Version® Anglicized, NIV® Copyright © 1979, 1984, 2011 by Biblica, Inc.® Used by permission. All rights reserved worldwide. Scripture quotations marked MSG are taken from *The Message*, copyright © 1993, 1994, 1995, 1996, 2000, 2001, 2002 by Eugene H. Peterson. Used by permission of NavPress. All rights reserved. Represented by Tyndale House Publishers, Inc. Quotations marked BCP are taken from The Book of Common Prayer of 1662, the rights of which are vested in the Crown in perpetuity within the United Kingdom, are reproduced by permission of Cambridge University Press, Her Majesty's Printers.

Unless otherwise stated, photographs are by Jo Ind and Rob Lainchbury. Photo on p. 96 © marta-dzedyshko-1042863/pexels.com; photo on p. 142 © teona-swift/pexels.com. Used with permission.

Every effort has been made to trace and contact copyright owners for material used in this resource. We apologise for any inadvertent omissions or errors, and would ask those concerned to contact us so that full acknowledgement can be made in the future.

A catalogue record for this book is available from the British Library

Printed and bound by Ashford Colour Press

Death & Life

A church's guide
to exploring mortality

Joanna Collicutt, Jo Ind,
Victoria Slater and Alison Webster

Contents

About this book 6

Good practice..12

Thinking about mortality..16

Talking about mortality..22
    Principles 23
    Creative workshop 24

Living well in the light of mortality 38
    Sermon starters.. 41
    Bible studies 54
    Reflective sessions 77
    Prayer stations 89

Preparing for death 104
    Running a Well-Prepared course 105

Background reading 144

Acknowledgements 148

Death and Life prayer...150

Notes 152

About this book

Why this resource?

As a society, we aren't good at talking about death, and as individuals we may try and avoid thinking about it. This is made easier for us by the fact that these days the process of death has been largely handed over to professionals, so we rarely witness it, and many of us can go through life without ever having seen the body of a person who has died. The Covid pandemic has made surprisingly little difference to this in our collective consciousness. In many ways, it is reasonable for us to try and keep our distance from death, for it is a deeply threatening reality:

> It is fundamentally uncontrollable and unpredictable;
>
> It involves (unknown and perhaps extreme) physical pain and discomfort;
>
> It separates loved ones;
>
> It is undergone alone;
>
> It interrupts our plans and projects, and may make life seem pointless;
>
> It seems to annihilate those who undergo it.

Yet we cannot deal with the threat by avoiding it forever, and society is beginning to wake up to this fact. 'Bucket lists' have entered the national vocabulary; death cafés are fairly commonplace; and organisations such as the National Council for Palliative Care (ncpc.org.uk), Compassion in Dying (compassionindying.org.uk) and the Dying Matters Coalition (hospiceuk.org/our-campaigns/dying-matters) have brought the topic of death and the process of dying out of the shadows and into the public arena. It turns out that many people, especially older people, would value an opportunity to talk frankly about what is sometimes known as 'the last taboo'.

The role of churches

While the religious landscape is changing, churches and faith communities have an important role to play in offering both pastoral care and theological accompaniment to the dying and the bereaved. There is a challenge and an opportunity for churches and faith communities to (re)claim their role – to re–weave religion and death.[1]

Churches have traditionally been the place for funerals, but this is becoming less common, as an increasing range of alternative providers enter the marketplace. Between 2013 and 2022, the Church of England's Life Events project developed resources to enrich and refresh funeral ministry. These included materials for a Christian equivalent of a death café – Grave Talk (churchofengland.org/life-events/funerals). There is also a Roman Catholic web-based equivalent of the mediaeval book called the *Ars Moriendi* produced by St Mary's University – The Art of Dying Well (artofdyingwell.org). But, perhaps surprisingly, churches have not invested a great deal of effort in addressing questions of mortality (in contrast, for example, with their concerns around sexuality and gender).

Ironically, this may have something to do with institutional churches' fear of their own mortality. A few years ago, a senior church administrator remarked that churches face a numerical decline because 'we haven't found a way to halt death'. But, of course, in Jesus we have just that. The message that Christians proclaim and try to live out is one of life in the midst of death and hope in the midst of loss. For 'I came that they may have life and have it abundantly' (John 10:10). We have something significant to say about all this.

Nevertheless, it can be hard to communicate traditional Christian teaching on this vital topic in ways that make sense to 21st-century folk, even if they are regular churchgoers. The central truth of our faith seems to be the one that is hardest to communicate. We need to re-learn how to have proper conversations about it.

This book contains resources to help us begin the conversation and then dive deeper into this matter of death and life.

Background

In 2003, my (Joanna's) mother suffered a serious heart attack and at one point was given 48 hours to live. As is so often the case with older people, her 'death trajectory' turned out to be more complicated: she lived another seven years. She spent those years well, regularly visiting churches to pray privately and prepare herself spiritually for the end of her earthly life.

Whether by choice or not, she did this alone and unsupported. When I shared this with a senior church leader, he reflected, 'It's a great shame that the churches don't do more to help people with this important task!' The seed of an idea had been planted.

Meanwhile, I had taken up the post of adviser for spiritual care for older people for the diocese of Oxford. I was reflecting on what 'spiritual care' actually means, and how churches might go beyond tending to the physical and emotional well-being of older people (important though this is) and offer something distinctively Christian.

I had another significant conversation, this time with a young Jewish woman, who pointed out that, unlike many religious traditions, Christianity does not offer a model for how to grow old gracefully; its founder, Jesus of Nazareth, 'lived fast and died young'. This conversation drew my attention back to something I had not noticed before: the New Testament presents older people as faithful prophets rather than knowledgeable sages. The Christian faith sees old age not as a dignified decline into oblivion, but the urgent run-up to its ultimate goal, stepping through the gateway of death to resurrection life.

Yet, outside of Easter services, there didn't seem to be much talk of this sort of thing going on in church circles. Unlike baptism and marriage, there were hardly any courses laid on by churches to prepare folk for this ultimate life event. So, in 2012 I delivered one myself. It was very successful and became a pilot for what turned but to be a much bigger project run jointly by Oxford Diocese and Ripon College Cuddesdon. This ran from 2014 to 2018 and was supported in part by a generous grant from the Henry Smith Charity. It is out of this more substantial project – gathering stories, recording good practice, identifying needs, doing theological reflection – that this resource has been developed.

Evidence

The resources and principles for good practice that we have created are rooted in evidence of their effectiveness.

We are used to the idea of 'evidence-based' practice in health care. If you go into hospital for an operation, you rightly want to know the possible risks and benefits of the procedure based on research evidence. We are much less used to thinking about evidence in relation to spiritual care, but it is just as important.

It is simply unethical to waste our own and other people's time and energy doing something that at best will make no difference to them and at worst might do them some harm. In the area of death and dying, there is a small but real risk of doing harm – of giving people false information, of opening up cans of worms that were better left shut, of taking insufficient care of our and their emotional vulnerabilities. Understanding these risks should not put us off this area of work; instead, it should motivate us to ensure that we engage in best practice. And the basis for best practice is research evidence.

The resources in this book have come out of a process documented in two publications in peer-reviewed journals: *Working with Older People*[2] and *Practical Theology*.[3] It is an example of theological 'action research'. Action research is used in the human sciences, especially in the areas of health and social care. It:

> Is context-based, addressing real life problems;
>
> Aimed at collaboration between participants and researchers;
>
> Sees diversity and complexity as enriching rather than distracting;
>
> Has a recursive structure, generating new actions from its findings, which themselves lead to new research questions.

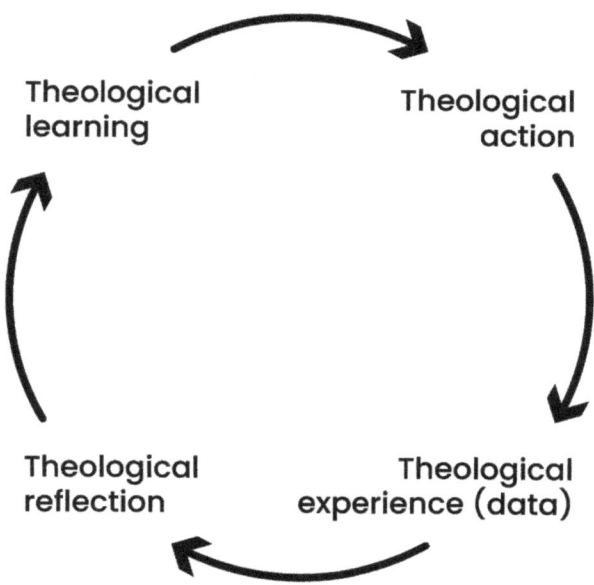

Diagram 1: The recursive nature of health and social care

This research took us into three areas, all of which are covered in this book:

1 How to think about mortality in the light of the gospel;
2 How to talk well about mortality and prepare for our own death;
3 How to live the whole of life well in the light of our mortality.

But before getting started on them, it is important to pause and consider some guidelines for good practice in this area.

Good practice

Guidelines for good practice

It takes (at least) two

Ensure you have one or two people to share the work

Even if you're simply preaching a one-off sermon on death and dying, it's important to have some support in place to help you reflect on what you are trying to achieve and the impact (intended or unintended) of what you say.

If you're running a group event that involves face-to-face conversations about death and dying, this will be even more important because:

> A person in your group may become ill or distressed;
>
> It helps to manage group dynamics and to share the practical tasks;
>
> The facilitators can support each other and offer constructive feedback and peer supervision. One function of supervision is to be 'critical friends', holding each other accountable;
>
> You can pray for each other.

It's also important to know your limits and to identify someone whose advice you can seek if you think you may be getting out of your depth, for example, a health care professional or hospital/hospice chaplain, who is willing to be available at the end of a phone.

In confidence

Respect and confidentiality are fundamental principles

There should be clear rules about confidentiality. This will depend on the context of your work. For example, a discussion after a sermon is essentially a public event, but a specific course or workshop that individuals have signed up for is more private. In these latter cases, it is important to set some agreed confidentiality boundaries at the beginning of sessions. To feel safe, people need to know that what they have shared will remain within the group and that their requests to remain anonymous will be respected.

But if someone discloses a safeguarding-related issue, you should seek advice from your church safeguarding officer, or if that is not possible, from your local adult safeguarding board.

If you are keeping records (hard copy or electronic), they should comply with the General Data Protection Regulations (ico.org.uk/for-organisations). Any notes that are taken should be anonymised, e.g. 'Mrs X' instead of name.

Look after yourself

Be prepared for your work to bring up difficult feelings in yourself

Working in the area of death and dying can be particularly challenging if you have been recently bereaved or are going through a difficult time. Even 'old' losses can unexpectedly come back to the surface when we start to explore this area. So make sure that the time is right for you. And whatever your situation, try to ensure the following things are in place:

> Awareness that working with this material might raise issues for you personally and that you might need to take some time to process what arises in a way that is helpful to you. Keeping a journal may be helpful here.
>
> Enough time to prepare for the event and to process the thoughts and feelings that are likely to be shared with you. It is not a good idea to try to squeeze conversations about death in between other appointments.
>
> Resources to sustain you. You may find it helpful to schedule a relaxing activity such as a walk, a meditation or something creative for yourself before or after these conversations.
>
> Supervision and support. Someone you know and trust to talk things through with and share your feelings.

Go the distance

Provide support that goes beyond the duration of the event

A course or workshop on death and dying may put people in touch with deep things in their lives. This means it may be some time after the event that a person feels the need to talk with someone, and it's important that there's a named person they can contact who will listen to them and provide appropriate pastoral support. You need to ensure that:

> It is made clear that there's a named person who people can contact for pastoral support;
>
> People know how to contact that person;
>
> People know that they can contact that person at any time after the event.

Who the appropriate pastoral contact is will vary according to the context. It may be one of the facilitators or, if the course or workshop is being run with a preformed group, it may be the group convenor who is the named person.

Where to find help

Age UK: ageuk.org.uk

Art of Dying Well: artofdyingwell.org

Church of England funerals: churchofengland.org/life-events/funerals

Compassion in Dying: compassionindying.org.uk

Funeral Guide: funeralguide.co.uk

The National Council for Palliative Care: ncpc.org.uk

For background reading, see p. 144.

Thinking about mortality

Living well in the last days: a theological reflection

Death and loss are right at the heart of the Christian story

The Bible is full of stories of death and life, grief and joy, finding and losing. The New Testament is centred on the death of Jesus. More than that, the first generation of Christians who had known him, and whose witness is the basis of the gospels, were bereaved communities. They had lived through the trauma of losing him to a dreadful death, had experienced a brief reunion and then had lost him again. They continued to face adversity, physical danger and rejection of their message.

Yet these communities and the writings that emerged from them were infused with hope, grounded in the certainty that Jesus had been through death and come out the other side victorious, robbing it of its power to inflict dread. Jesus had 'passed through the heavens' (Hebrews 4:14). This gives him a special authority on the subject, born of experience:

> *A Zen master, asked by his student to tell him about death, said he knew nothing about the topic. 'How can that be?' said the student. 'A master must surely have knowledge of such things.' To which the master replied, 'Ah, but I am not a dead Zen master.'*[4]

Jesus, in contrast, is a 'dead-and-alive' master who has returned 'from the dead' (Luke 16:30). He is uniquely placed to show us how to face the prospect of our own death and to undergo it when it comes; and his resurrection is a first fruit or seal of ours (1 Corinthians 15:20). So, as we think about our own mortality, as in everything else, we have a model presented to us in Jesus.

Following Jesus in his attitude to those who are bereaved

Jesus' response to bereavement comes out of sight and insight. Luke tells us that Jesus felt compassion for a widow who had lost her son because he looked at her properly: 'When the Lord saw her, his heart went out to her and he said, "Don't cry"' (Luke 7:13, NIV). More famously, Jesus wept at the tomb of his friend Lazarus, but what evoked his tears seems to have been not just a sense of his own loss but deep empathy for his friend, Mary and her companions: 'When Jesus saw her weeping and the Jews who came with her also weeping, he was greatly disturbed in spirit and deeply moved' (John 11:33). In both these cases, Jesus goes on, driven by his compassion, to raise the dead.

He does something less dramatic when he notices his own mother at the foot of the cross beginning her own journey of bereavement: 'When

Jesus saw his mother and the disciple whom he loved standing beside her, he said to his mother, "Woman, here is your son." Then he said to the disciple, "Here is your mother"' (John 19:26–27). Here he looks with insight into his mother's needs and with foresight into the way those needs can be met.

To follow Jesus is to notice people who are bereaved, to respond with empathy and compassion, and to act to address their practical, emotional or spiritual needs.

Following Jesus in preparing for our death

Facing not seeking

Jesus faced up to his death and spent a good deal of time trying to prepare his disciple for its reality. They resisted this reality (Matthew 16:21–26), but Luke tells us that Jesus was resolute and readied himself for the challenge (Luke 9:51; 13:33).

Yet Jesus did not seek death for its own sake. For a time, he was careful to avoid arrest in Jerusalem by using safe houses, but when he understood that his hour had come, he went out to meet his foes (John 13:31). Even then, the gospel writers are at pains to make it clear that death was the last thing Jesus wanted. If he could have avoided it, he would have (Matthew 26:39 and parallels). He loved life and he understood the horror of death.

Comfort and provision for those left behind

Part of Jesus' facing of his death is the care he gave to those he would be leaving behind. John 13—16 is an extended farewell in which Jesus expresses his love and intimacy with his followers; models the way of life they are to embrace in mutual love and service; offers them an image of attachment in the discourse on the true vine; and promises them the Spirit to comfort them in their loss. In the synoptic gospels, Jesus offers the breaking of bread as a way both to remember him and to re-member themselves as a body (Luke 22:19).

Receiving care with good grace

Throughout his life, Jesus entrusted himself to others: to Mary and Joseph through his childhood, to the seamanship of the disciples to escape from the crush of the crowds (Mark 3:9), to the female followers who provided for him (Luke 8:2–3), to the hospitality of those who opened their homes to him (Luke 10:38) and to the goodwill of the Samaritan to give him a drink of water from the well (John 4:6–7).

As his death approached, he praised a woman (probably Mary of Bethany) for recognising it and anointing his body for burial (Matthew 26:12; John 12:7), describing her action as beautiful or fitting. Later, in Gethsemane, he seemed genuinely to desire the presence of his disciples to uphold him in prayer and comfort him by their solidarity.

To follow Jesus is to face up to the prospect of our own death, to make provision for those left behind and to learn to receive the care and support of others with grace and joy.

Following Jesus in undergoing death

In a theological sense, Jesus' death might be seen as heroic, but in a human sense it was full of pathos – literally 'pathetic' – and this is also recognised theologically in the image of Jesus as a lamb who was slain. Jesus wept not just in empathy with others but at his own fate that was the natural consequence of his rejection by those he loved (Luke 19:41). The writer to the Hebrews says that Jesus cried in Gethsemane in his anguished struggle of discernment (Hebrews 5:7). And, of course, he cried out to his Father on the cross (Matthew 27:46).

As W. H. Vanstone has pointed out in his book *The Stature of Waiting*,[5] when the time was right Jesus moved from active ministry into his 'passion', a period in which he was entirely passive, treated as an object, and – in human terms – without agency (Matthew 27:42). He underwent an agonising physical process in which, among other things, he became dehydrated (John 19:28).

We might say, then, that at the moment of his death, he:

> Was utterly under the control of others and the physical process;
>
> Was in physical agony;
>
> Experienced separation from his Father;
>
> Had been deserted by most of his followers and underwent it alone;
>
> Asked the question, 'Why?';
>
> Was effectively annihilated for 24+ hours.

Jesus' death embraced all those aspects of death that make it such a threatening prospect set out on p. 7. He has faced all of its horrors.

Jesus' death was thus an ordinary human death, undergone extraordinarily well, authentically and in an exemplary way. Yet much more was going on. Jesus, the craftsman, was doing something creative; Jesus, the divine Saviour, was transforming death itself. This is hinted at in his cry to his Father, framed in the opening words of Psalm 22, a psalm that journeys through deep darkness and suffering into a transformed sense of God's goodness and sovereignty. Even as he hung on the cross, he made space to re-member the human lives of his mother, the beloved disciple and a convicted criminal who hung alongside him.

Jesus' death was uniquely sacrificial in the sense that it was life-giving for all humanity. He understood it to be the culmination of his mission (John 19:30). He reflected that a grain of wheat falls into the earth in order to bear much fruit (John 12:24). Death and dying are seen to be about creation and re-creation.

As followers of Jesus, we join in that creative and life-giving work through lives marked by sacrifice and praise, and through it we participate in his glorious resurrection.

To follow Jesus is to approach our living and dying as creative acts that bring fullness of life to ourselves and others, to be aware of the time when possessions, agency and treasured relationships are to be let go and to trust the ultimate goodness of God. Our deaths do not need to be heroic; we do not need to be strong; we can cry out to God in pain and distress, and we can be sure that he is with us.

The importance of the last days

Christianity began its life as a renewal movement within Judaism and, crucially, was based on the conviction that a new age was dawning, that the world was standing at a threshold that marked a flip between the existing political status quo and a new inverted and subversive reality (the 'kingdom of God'). The gospels only mention three older adults – Zachariah and Elizabeth (Luke 1) and Anna (Luke 2) – carefully positioned before the beginning of Jesus' adult ministry, as if marking the transition from an obsolete generation. Much of Jesus' conflict with the authorities is an intergenerational conflict between an up-and-coming young man and the establishment of elders.

Yet Zechariah, Elizabeth and Anna themselves subvert expectations about older adults: Luke presents all three as looking eagerly towards the future, sitting lightly to the past, rather than as repositories of wisdom based on previous life experience. This is also true of Simeon (who is often assumed to be an older person). They are all liminal people who respond to the next generation in hope rather than fear.

In Acts, Luke returns to this theme and, quoting the prophet Joel, indicates a special place for older adults as the new age dawns:

> *In the last days it will be, God declares, that I will pour out my Spirit upon all flesh, and your sons and your daughters shall prophesy, and your young men shall see visions, and your old men shall dream dreams.*
> ACTS 2:17 (SEE ALSO JOEL 2:28)

The phrase 'the last days' refers to historical ages, but it can also be creatively read in relation to the end of life. This means that people in their last days on this earth may have the potential to be 'eschatological visionaries' poised on the threshold between this life and a life to come, this earth and a heavenly home (Hebrews 11:14).

To put it another way, we might consider the last days as a 'thin place'[6] or a mountain top that affords new vistas, as yet hidden over the horizon from the young, fit and well. The phrase 'over the hill' can thus be read in a positive light, inviting the question of what might be learnt if attention were paid to the stories such visionaries might have to tell.

This means that the church may have much to learn from those who are living in their last days, whether they are old or young. Working with those who are close to death will then involve receiving from them as much as giving to them.

It also means that the lessons learned in the last days need to become integrated into the whole lifespan of faith, so that people of all ages and stages of faith can learn to live well in the light of mortality. For example, BRF Ministries has produced Messy Church resources for young and old to begin to talk about death together (find out more at brfonline.org.uk/seriouslymessy).

Talking about mortality

Principles

Our work on enabling people to talk about death and dying is based on some fundamental principles that have emerged from our research:

People should be met where they are. This means taking their beliefs and concerns seriously by listening attentively to them and expecting to learn something. It means bringing God's story into conversation with their story rather than telling people all the answers.

Practice should be positive. Our practice in this area should be effective and not be harmful. We believe in reflecting on our work and, as far as is possible, developing evidence-based practice.

Reflecting on death is for everyone. People of all ages and states of health, not just those who are frail or terminally ill, should be encouraged to consider their mortality and engage with Christian teaching on the resurrection. We see this as an issue of discipleship.

We need to receive the wisdom of 'the last days'. The final phases of life for both old and young can be places of potential learning, growth and prophetic vision from which others can learn. This means gathering stories, documenting insights and encouraging creative expression – receiving wisdom, not just giving pastoral care.

Creative workshop

A safe, creative space for people to express stories of death and dying in their own ways

The workshop is:

> Approximately two hours long – but can be flexible;
>
> For up to 15 adults;
>
> Formulated to encourage creative responses to death and dying;
>
> Designed as a stand-alone event;
>
> Not heavy with Christian content and therefore adaptable for use with people of other faiths or no specific faith.

Purpose and outcomes

Before embarking on a workshop, be clear about its purpose and the expected outcomes.

Purpose

The overall purpose of a workshop is:

> To enable participants to get in touch with their feelings about death and dying;
>
> To enable participants to explore and articulate the meanings they bring to this reality;
>
> To listen to participants' experiences and their personal and theological understandings;

> To generate and share stories, images and 'bottom-up' theologies from experience in order to inform and feed the life of that particular Christian community.

Outcomes

For workshop leaders, the outcomes of a workshop can include:

> Deeper insight and understanding of where people are in their lives to inform ministerial practice;
>
> Deeper understanding of their own theologies or worldviews;
>
> Enrichment of their personal, spiritual and professional lives through being open to receive wisdom and insight from others.

Outline structure

The workshop is designed to last for two hours including a refreshment break.

> **Welcome (10 minutes).** This includes setting ground rules such as confidentiality, respect and self-responsibility and a brief outline of the session and its purpose to ensure people feel safe and know what to expect.
>
> **Reflection (10 minutes).** Listening to a poem and a song to begin quietly thinking about mortality.
>
> **Silence (5 minutes).** This gives people time to reflect and to feel their own responses to what they have encountered.
>
> **Discussion (10 minutes).** This can be done either in pairs or as a group. It gives an opportunity to discuss what has been encountered and what it has evoked.
>
> **Refreshment break (15 minutes).**
>
> **Creative engagement (40 minutes).** An opportunity to write a legacy card, make a collage, paint a picture or respond to reflection cards.
>
> **Sharing (20 minutes).** Time to share responses and creative expressions.
>
> **Drawing the threads together (5 minutes).** An opportunity to draw out the main questions, themes, insights and concerns that have been voiced.
>
> **Ending with prayer (5 minutes).**

Setting up

Certain things need to be in place to create an environment in which participants can feel supported and safe. This will ensure that everyone involved has as positive and enriching an experience as possible.

An ethically responsible approach

Before leading a workshop ensure you:

> Provide a participant information sheet (p. 34) so that people are clear about the purpose of the workshop; its structure and length; anonymity and boundaries; and who is running it and how to contact them.
>
> Obtain the contact details for participants in case you need to be in touch following the workshop. These details should be obtained and held in compliance with the current Data Protection Act.
>
> Be clear about what will happen to the work that people produce. It should be treated with the same respect as anything that is spoken or written. You may like to decide with the group what to do. People may simply want to take it home with them. However, if you want to be able to share either the original work or photographs with others, you will need to ask permission from individuals to do that, including a clear agreement as to whether or not they want it to be attributed.
>
> Ensure that any notes taken are not attributable.

Workshop facilitators

It's important that there are two workshop facilitators, for the following reasons:

> When one person is giving input, the other can be aware of what is going on in the group, attend to practicalities and offer any support that may be required.
>
> One of the facilitators can take notes. Notes might provide theological reflection material for a leadership team.
>
> It provides a greater breadth of resources and experience.
>
> It provides mutual support during the workshop.
>
> It provides the opportunity to debrief after the workshop as part of self-care and to enrich learning and evaluation.

Ongoing pastoral support

A workshop on death and dying may put people in touch with deep personal or existential issues. It is important that if people wish to talk with someone following the workshop, there is a named person they can contact for pastoral support. You need to ensure that people know how to contact that person, should they wish to do so, and that they can do so at any point after the workshop.

Who, when, where

Think carefully about who to invite to a workshop and the best time and place to hold it.

Who?

People encounter death and dying at any age, be it through personal illness, tragedy or loss or through media saturated with images and stories of death.

This workshop is suitable for any adult who has not been recently bereaved who would like to reflect on their personal engagement with mortality and its existential, spiritual and theological implications.

Who you invite will depend on your context. There may be a church or community group that would like to do the workshop, or you may want to issue a general invitation to people in your church, deanery, parish, or the wider local community.

When?

The workshop can be run at any time of the year. However, you might like to tie it in either with a wider discussion about death and dying, for example a sermon series or Bible studies, or with a particular time in the church's year, such as Advent, Lent or Easter.

In practical terms, when you decide to hold the workshop will depend on the demographic of those taking part. For example, if people have work, family or care commitments, it may be difficult for them to come to a weekday afternoon session, whereas this may be a good time for people without such commitments. Some older people may be reluctant to turn out for an evening session, especially during the dark winter months.

Wording for publicity

It's rare to have the opportunity to come together with other people to reflect on living and dying and the fact that every one of us will have to do our own dying at some point. This workshop offers a safe and enjoyable forum in which we can reflect on some of the fundamental questions that our mortality poses.

> What does mortality mean for how I live or want to live my life?
>
> What do I really believe?
>
> What really matters, in the end?

There will be reflection, music, poetry, creative activities and sharing.

Materials

This is a (non-definitive) list of the basic items you will need to deliver a workshop.

You will need three large tables for the different creative activities. People may choose to sit and work round a table or to take materials and work elsewhere.

For the writing/wisdom legacy card table

A variety of paper and card of different sizes, textures and colours; a variety of pens and pencils of different colours; reflection cards; a selection of poems about death and life to provide inspiration.

For the collage table

Different sizes of plain and coloured paper; scissors, glue sticks; a selection of materials such as tissue paper, ribbon, glitter, felt, coloured card – the more varied the better; a selection of magazines from which people can cut out words and images for their collage.

For the art/drawing table

A broad selection of crayons, pastels, pens, paints and paper; brushes and water pots if using watercolour paint; kitchen paper for cleaning any mess.

Evaluation

The evaluation of your workshop, by both participants and facilitators, is an important part of the work.

By participants

A short, anonymous evaluation form (pp. 35–36) can be given to people to fill in at an appropriate point before they leave the session.

This gives people the chance to feed back about their experience of the workshop and to raise any particular issues. It's also a learning tool for the facilitator and, if the comments are positive, can be a source of encouragement and even inspiration.

By facilitators

After the workshop, it is important for facilitators to meet informally while the experience is still fresh. This provides space to debrief and to talk about:

> How they feel about the experience of facilitating the workshop;
>
> The things that went well that need to be captured;
>
> Questions and concerns that have arisen and need to be addressed;
>
> Things that need to be learned and used to inform subsequent workshops;
>
> Any issues that have arisen for the group or individuals;
>
> Any follow-up that is needed.

It's also recommended that facilitators make time to write up their own reflections on the session, including their own responses and anything that has been evoked for them. This is part of being a good reflective practitioner and will maximise personal and professional learning and development. The insights gained can be used to inform the running of subsequent workshops or courses.

Checklist

Before you start your workshop, run through this checklist to ensure you're good to go:

1. Have participants received an information sheet?
2. Is the venue accessible and comfortable?
3. Can refreshments be made available at the venue?
4. Are there tables to use at the venue?
5. Have you got copies of the poem and song lyrics, including large print copies as required?
6. Have you got the practical resources such as:

   > stickers for names
   >
   > Bibles in a range of translations
   >
   > pens/pencils/pastilles/paints etc
   >
   > brushes
   >
   > cups/glasses to use for water
   >
   > various sizes of paper

> newspaper to cover tables
>
> kitchen roll for spills/hands
>
> scissors
>
> magazines for collage
>
> music set-up?

7 Do you have the names and contact details of participants held in compliance with the current Data Protection Act in case there are things you need to follow up with people after the workshop?

8 Is there a named person that people can contact for pastoral support? Do people know who they can contact and how to do so?

Detailed workshop content

1 Welcome

Suggested text for introducing the workshop:

We're surrounded by images of death and dying in the media and the Christian tradition has at its centre the story of the life and death of Jesus Christ and the meanings that his friends and disciples have brought to those events down the centuries. Yet people rarely have opportunity to come together to reflect on their own living and dying and on the fact that every one of us will have to do our own dying at some point. Although this workshop offers some resources and stories of the meanings that writers and artists have brought to the ultimate question of what death and life means, it's meant to be an opportunity for you to reflect on what it means for yourself – and that might be very different from what it means to others past and present.

This is an opportunity to ask yourself some of the questions that the fact of our mortality poses to each one of us: what do I really believe? What does death and dying mean for how I live my life or want to live my life? What really matters, in the end? Of course, it may be that, as for many if not most of us, there are a lot of things you don't know, questions that have no immediate answers and that just have to be lived.

The workshop is designed to provide you with resources that we hope may help and inspire you in this reflective process but the important thing is to listen to yourself – not to who you think you should be, but to who you authentically are, maybe with many doubts, fears and anxieties – and to accept where you are with things as the only place to be.

It may be that for you, the workshop will be an exploration and that it is only as you start to do something, to make a mark on a piece of paper or choose a colour, that you can begin to know the truth of things for yourself.

The important thing to know is that anything you express in whatever way is valuable and will be valued as unique to you; it is not about being 'good' at anything. It is also important to know that confidentiality will be taken seriously; everyone's confidence will be honoured and we will treat each other and the contributions we make with respect.

Any creative work that people produce will be treated with the same respect and degree of confidentiality as anything that is spoken or written. You are welcome to take your work home with you. If you don't want to do that, we will destroy it once the workshop has finished. We won't share it with anyone without asking your permission.

The structure is simple: after a short introduction we will listen to a song. This will be followed by time for reflection and discussion about what you have encountered before a short break. After the break, we'll have time to engage in some creative work before we share our responses together.

2 Reflection

You can begin the reflection with words like these:

The Christian tradition teaches that in his life, death and resurrection, Jesus inaugurated 'the end times'. This is a phrase usually associated with the eschaton – the time when the current age ends, the new age begins and the values of earth give way to the values of heaven. Yet, in our busy, daily lives it is not easy to keep sight of this; most of the time, it feels as though the days, weeks and months will just keep on rolling by. However, as death comes closer through illness, loss, tragedy or the ageing process, we all enter our own 'end times'; we approach the threshold of eternity and this may focus our minds and hearts on the question of how to live well in this period of our lives.

All the great spiritual and religious traditions recognise the importance of paying attention to the fact that we are mortal and will die. St Benedict, for example, advised his monks to keep death always before their eyes. Why? What is to be gained by keeping in mind our own mortality?

Deep inside each one of us, there is a place where we know we will die. Paradoxically, it is this awareness that binds us to every other human being and pushes us not to be content with living on the surface of things and people but to enter the heart and depth of them. When we encounter death or loss, either our own or that of a loved one, we are presented with the essential questions:

> Who am I?
>
> What is my life for?
>
> Have I loved well?
>
> Have I truly lived/am I truly living the life that I have been given?
>
> What is my legacy to this life?

> What do I really believe?
>
> What do I hope for at death and beyond?

These are big questions and life is so full for most of us that we rarely take time to stop and reflect on them in any depth.

Introduce and read the poem 'When Death Comes' by Mary Oliver.

('When Death Comes' can be found in *New and Selected Poems*, Beacon Press. There are also versions of it on the internet.)

Pause briefly to allow participants to appreciate the poem.

Jeremy Taylor, a seventeenth century bishop, wrote in his book *Holy Dying* (1651) that, 'Dying is an art, and to be learned by men (sic) in health.' But how do we learn to die? Taking time today to think about death and dying and to let these kinds of questions question us is part of that learning. Becoming more deeply aware of our own mortality can enable us to find new richness and meaning in our lives, perhaps a reordering of our priorities, a deeper realisation of what really matters – and it is not usually the possession of material goods! Moreover, reflecting on our own living and dying brings us up against who we really are before God, beyond the self we usually project into the world.

So, we consciously encounter the great paradox that reflecting on our own mortality calls us back to focus on what it means for us to be fully alive. As St Irenaeus said in the second century, 'The glory of God is a human being fully alive.'

This workshop is an opportunity for us to respond to the awareness we hold together that we are 'living in the end times' and to use that as an opportunity to explore how to live well, how to be fully alive.

We can do that by asking ourselves some simple but profound questions:

> Looking back what do I think my legacy will be? What have been the significant events, relationships and encounters that have made my story meaningful? What do I need to let go of from the past and what do I need to cherish and hold on to? What would I like my legacy to be?
>
> What makes life precious, fulfilling and fruitful now?
>
> What do I hope for at death and beyond?

Introduce and play the song 'For a Dancer' by Jackson Browne.

One man's reflection on the meaning of life in the light of the death of a loved one. (A version of this song is available on YouTube).

Follow with a short silence for reflection.

We'll now have a time of silence, to pause and reflect on your responses at this point. This gives people time to reflect and to feel their own responses to what they have encountered.

Invite the participants to talk to each other.

It can be done either in pairs or as a group. It gives an opportunity to discuss what has been encountered and what it has evoked. Give people the opportunity to carry on talking over tea and coffee.

3 Creative engagement

Invite participants to take part in one of several creative activities that are set out on different tables in the space.

> Creating wisdom legacy cards. Write on a card something learned through life that a person would like to pass on to others, their own wisdom legacy or something from scripture that is important to them.
>
> Collage. Use the materials to create a picture of your feelings about life and death.
>
> Art. Draw or paint a picture in response to what you have heard.
>
> Theological reflection. Offer a set of reflection cards, available to purchase from **brfonline.org.uk/death-and-life-cards**.

4 Sharing

Invite the participants to share with the group some of their creative expressions and reflections.

5 Drawing the threads together

Articulate the main questions, themes, insight and concerns that have been voiced.

6 Prayer

End with a prayer, if appropriate.

Information for participants

Thank you for taking part in this workshop.

The aim of the workshop is to help people to reflect creatively on death and dying and on what this reality means for the way in which we live our lives. It offers a chance to reflect on some of the questions that our mortality poses such as: what really matters in the end? What do I really believe? The workshop will help us to learn from the experiences, unique stories and wisdom that people share as we reflect together on how to live well in the light of our mortality.

The workshop is intended to be a safe and enjoyable space in which to explore these issues. It will begin with a short reflection using music and poetry. Participants will then be invited to respond to this in conversation and a range of creative activities. The workshop will last approximately .... including a short break for refreshments.

We may share the themes, stories and creative work that emerges during the workshop to help others reflect on these issues, so, at times, there may be someone making notes. But we will not share any personal material without your permission.

We also ask participants to honour one another's confidentiality so that everyone can feel safe and at ease.

The sessions will be facilitated by..

If you would like more information or have questions, please do get in touch and we will be happy to discuss things with you.

We look forward to working with you and hope that you enjoy the workshop and find it a valuable and enriching experience.

Exploring death and life: workshop evaluation

Thank you for participating in this event.

It would be very helpful if you could let us know how you found it by answering the questions below:

Do you feel there is a need for events like these?

Not at all	To a small extent	To a moderate extent	To a great extent

To what extent has attending the event:

Made you more confident about issues around death and dying?

Not at all	To a small extent	To a moderate extent	To a great extent

Deepened or enriched your personal faith?

Not at all	To a small extent	To a moderate extent	To a great extent

PLEASE TURN OVER

Was the format helpful?
If not, what would you have liked to be different?

Were the venue and time helpful?
If not, what would have been more convenient?

What were the most helpful aspects of the event?

What were the least helpful aspects of the event?

**Are there things that you would like
to have been included?**

Do you have any further comments or suggestions?

THANK YOU FOR YOUR TIME

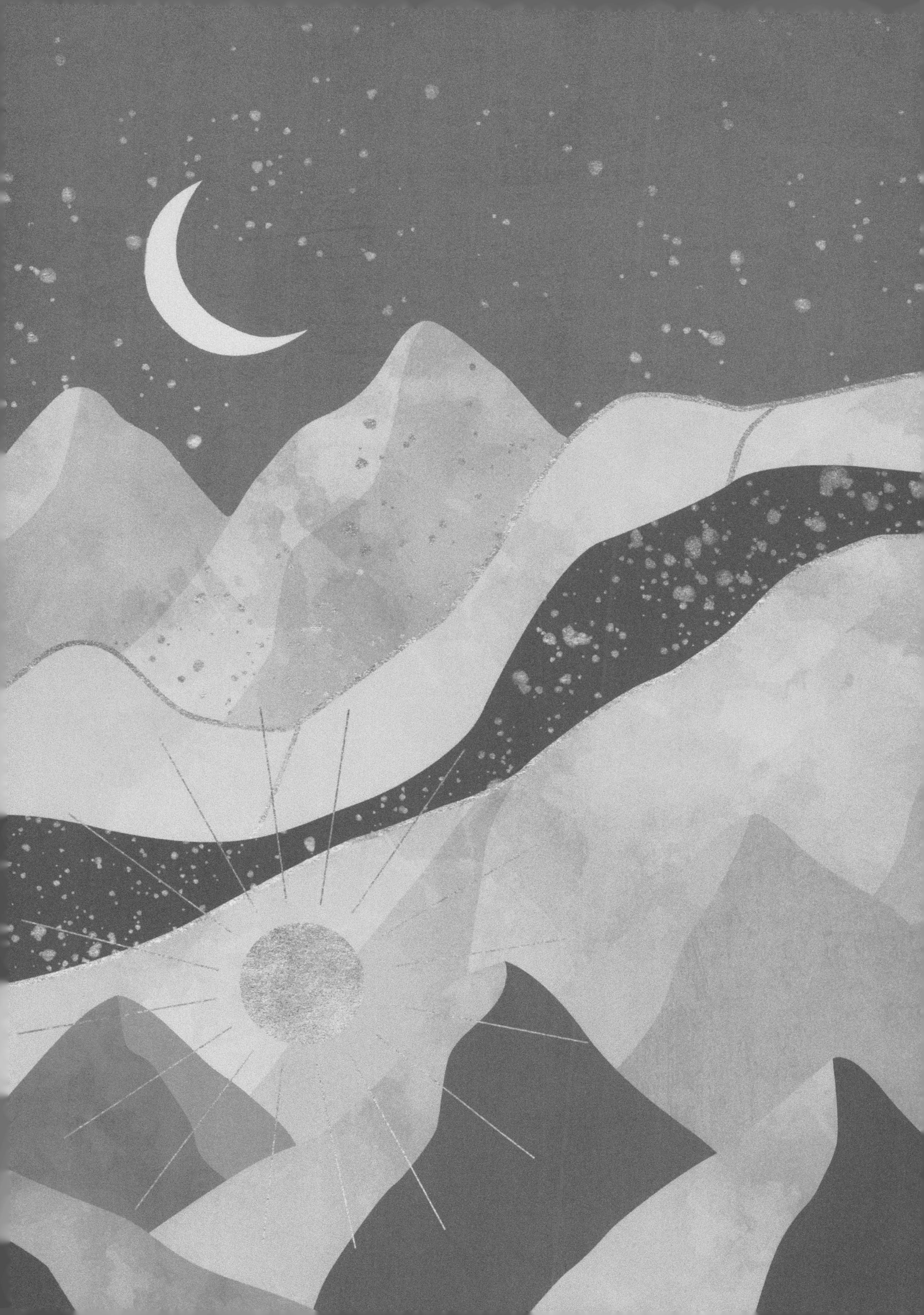

Living well in the light of mortality

Reflecting on our own death can enable us to live more fully in the here and now because the issues that come into sharp focus as death approaches turn out to be the same issues that are important in living life well.

In this section, which had additional input from Robert Glenny, Jeremy Brooks and Julie Mintern, we've identified six themes that seem to capture these important issues:

Loving

Life and death are bound up with love relationships. We are loved into being and we were bought for a price. True love puts the well-being of the other first, and so is sacrificial. The Christian calling is to love throughout life and to love most fully at the point of death.

Letting go

To die well is to let go graciously the very things we treasure and want to hold on to, trusting that something better awaits us. This is also in a smaller way our task throughout life.

Seeing

Death is about seeing beyond the veil, of dwelling in a greater, higher vision. In life we only catch glimpses of it, but these glimpses can expand our imagination, inspire us and give us hope and a truer vision for this world.

Growing

Death is about life-giving transformation, in which we are raised to our full stature in Christ. This is the end of a life-long process of transformation where we find that the most intense periods of growth may be in times of adversity.

Belonging

A deep paradox of death is that it is undergone alone but we are in company. This mirrors a paradox in life that our worth is determined both by our uniqueness as individuals and by our place as part of something bigger.

Hoping

Death is not the end. We are called to live our lives in this light.

We've created a range of resources to help people explore these themes. There are sermon starters; material for group Bible studies with each supported by a piece of visual art; ideas to craft more open reflective sessions incorporating poetry, music, visual art and a short meditative script; and prayer stations. They can be used in any combination and are summarised below.

Sermon starters

- Loving 41
- Letting go 43
- Seeing 45
- Growing 47
- Belonging 49
- Hoping 51

Bible studies

- Loving 54
- Letting go 58
- Seeing 62
- Growing 65
- Belonging 69
- Hoping 73

Reflective sessions

- Loving 77
- Letting go 79
- Seeing 81
- Growing 83
- Belonging 85
- Hoping 87

Prayer stations

- Loving 94
- Letting go 95
- Seeing 96
- Growing 97
- Belonging 98
- Hoping 99

You can see from this list that it's possible to pick a single item, for example a reflective session on the theme of growing. Or you could have a series of different types of events on one theme (choose the desired one from each section), for example 'letting go'. Or you could have just one type of event exploring all the themes (everything in one section), for example a series of sermons or a series of prayer stations. The prayer stations are particularly designed to work well together if combined into a prayer walk or as part of a labyrinth.

Sermon starters

Loving: sermon starter

1 Corinthians 13: the God of love and the love of God

Robert Glenny writes: This being a popular passage for wedding services, there is a familiar sermon that replaces the word 'love' between verses 4–8 with the name of Jesus. Look, says the preacher to the congregation, and see how Jesus is the supreme example of all of these qualities. Look at how Jesus and love are interchangeable. Today love is exalted as a virtue to be worshipped, but really it's Jesus who should receive that honour. And then they turn to face the couple and proclaim: if you invite Jesus into your marriage, your love will be stronger as a result. Don't rely on love; rely on Jesus.

It has always struck me, however, that the better description of Jesus comes in the first three verses. And frankly, whilst the Jesus I know is certainly kind, I'm not sure that I can read the gospels without discovering the character of someone who both insists on his own way and is more than irritable at the injustices of the world. Jesus speaks both in the language of heaven and earth. Jesus stands in, and echoes, and completes the prophetic line of those who have spoken God's word so that we may better hear it. Jesus astounded the temple as a young boy with his insight and his knowledge. And, perhaps definitively, Jesus does give away what little he possessed, and finally hands over his body. Naked Jesus enters this world. Naked he departs from it.

Now where does love fit? Are Christ and the virtue of love simply the same thing? If we say that God is love (1 John 4:8), must we also say that love is God? Not so. For Jesus' actions do not occur in a relational vacuum: had he done these virtuous and lovely acts without the driving, unceasing, eternal force of God's desperate love for God's creation, his life and death would have only resounded as a tuneless cymbal. Yes, Jesus loves, but more than that he shows us that God's very nature is a dance of love, a dance which is undeniably shaped towards us and which desires more than anything to include us.

Love, we discover, does not make any sense on its own. It is not an aspect of an individual's personality or character. It emerges, is discovered, cherished and valued only within relationships. What does it mean to be kind if there is no one to be kind towards? What virtue is there in not insisting on one's own way if no other way is offered? The true nature of these qualities that love describes (vv. 4–6) is that they are inherently sacrificial, laying aside the human condition of selfishness for love of another. Greater love has no one than this: that they lay down their life for their friend. Love is not God, but it does tell us why God does what he did in Christ. To love is to be prepared to sacrifice everything just to be in a relationship with the one you love.

We're reminded of this in the farewell discourse of John's gospel. 'Jesus knew that his hour had come to depart from this world and go to the Father. Having loved his own who were in the world, he loved them to the end' (John 13:1).

Here we sense, juxtaposed, the completeness of a life nearly over, and an expression of a love which will exist beyond death. As he comes to the realisation that time left with his friends is short, it is love that preoccupies Jesus. It is the motivation for the obedience he will show, and it will make the cross the definitive symbol of the sacrificial nature of God's love.

The final section from verse 9 onwards points towards the power that mutual love can have within a community. It is the movement from partiality to completeness; from youth to maturity. When we are in relationships which are formed by the security of love and trust, we allow ourselves to become vulnerable and intimate. The more one is loved the more one prepared to be known and the more one becomes known.

Mark Oakley has written that 'Faith intensifies rather than satisfies our longing for God'.[7] And so it is with love; becoming known deepens our desire to share more of ourselves. Catching a glimpse in the dim mirror heightens our yearning finally to see face to face. It is one of the great paradoxes of human existence that we want so very much to be loved for who we are, and yet we spend so much of our time shielding ourselves from being exposed to others. Those communities where we discover the love that allows us to be ourselves are the ones where we gain a foretaste of the completeness with which this passage ends.

Letting go: sermon starter

John 21:1–19: making a good ending

This meeting between Jesus and his disciples on the shore of Lake Galilee forms the final act of John's gospel. Here Jesus says both 'hello' and 'goodbye' to his followers, and we, as the readers of the gospel, realise that we too have reached the end of the story. We have read just enough to 'come to believe that Jesus is the Messiah, the Son of God, and that through believing… may have life in his name' (20:31).

Jesus stands on the lake-shore; we can imagine him waving to the fishermen just as he did once before when, according to the synoptic tradition, he called them from their nets. There is bread and fish baking on the fire (v. 9), and Jesus takes it and gives it to the disciples (v. 11), just as he had done on a previous memorable occasion (6:1). In his saying goodbye Jesus is returning and retelling the story of their life together, drawing the threads into a coherent whole full of resonances and interconnections.

The focal point for this going back is the charcoal fire, setting the stage for a reprise of Peter's threefold betrayal in the courtyard of the High Priest, where, as his hands were being warmed his heart turned cold with fear (18:17–27). We might describe Jesus' conversation with Peter over the fire with its threefold questioning as a process of reconciliation, followed by Peter's rehabilitation and re-commissioning. We might also be tempted to use the word 'forgiveness'. Is Jesus forgiving Peter?

The word 'forgiveness' occurs only once in John's gospel (20:23); it's clearly not a natural part of the writer's vocabulary. But it is a word that should give us pause for thought, because the Greek *aphiēmi*, usually translated 'forgive', literally means to 'let [it] go'. In going back to his past betrayal and re-working it through words of love, Jesus is offering Peter the chance to let go of it once and for all.

The past is let go of well; it will not return to haunt Peter. It must be so if Peter is to move forward into the next stage of his life and ministry. But we are then shown (v. 18) that the letting go is not to end here but is to continue into the future. Jesus reminds Peter that when he was young he could essentially do as he liked. He was nobody's slave (contrary to the popular stereotype of the uneducated impoverished fisherman, he was probably the head of a highly prosperous business); he had strength and vigour. He thus had both liberty (the freedom to do what he wished) and agency (the ability to do it).

Jesus lays out a future in which Peter will have to say goodbye to his liberty. He will end up somewhere he does not wish to go, and what's more he will not walk there under his own steam as a free and independent human being but will be taken there like a pet dog on a lead. He will have lost his liberty.

It's been traditional, and the text invites us, to read this as an allusion to Peter's eventual imprisonment and execution in Rome. But it actually reads more naturally as a broader reflection on old age. Just think, for example, about what it feels like to give up driving and become dependent on public transport, taxis, or lifts from friends. Or to move out of your own place into residential care, even the best-appointed sort of residential care. One often hears phrases like, 'We had to move Mum nearer to us as she wasn't coping anymore.' or 'The children moved us to be with them.' Or – most poignantly, 'Don't put me in a home!' In all of these sentences, the older person is the object or potential object of, often well-intentioned, actions of others. One older person remarked to me, 'I feel like a parcel waiting to be transported by Royal Mail.'

In these examples, the loss of liberty that comes with ageing is connected with a perceived loss of agency (the ability to be the captain of one's life), something that is referred to as 'capacity' in legal terms. And this, of course, affects other groups in addition to the elderly, such as those living with chronic health conditions, disabilities, or terminal illness.

All of these people are facing the process of letting go – of moving from doing to being, from knowing to unknowing, from deciding to waiting, from giving to receiving; and most of them are facing it reluctantly and with regret.

Yet, to return to the gospel, Peter's calling is to a loss of liberty and agency that mirrors that of his master's undergoing of his passion. His calling is to continue to serve and imitate his Lord right up to the end of his earthly life, even in the midst of its rigours and hardships as well as its joys. This is the life-long calling of all Christians. You don't retire from the life of faith; you keep on, even when what is intrinsic to keeping on is letting go.

This following Christ in letting go is ultimately and paradoxically what brings life from death and invests that life with meaning. John's gospel begins with a search for meaning by the disciples (and it assumes a search for meaning on the part of the reader); it ends with an invitation to make meaning by letting go. For Jesus' first words are 'What are you looking for?' (1:38) and his last words are 'Follow me!' (21:22). Between these utterances hang heaven and earth.

Seeing: sermon starter

Luke 24:13–36: the road to Emmaus as a 'thin place'

A number of writers, drawing on the Celtic tradition of the 'thin place' (a point where heaven and earth seem to come near to each other, v. 15), have suggested that these places are to be found not simply at sacred geographical sites or natural phenomena, but at points of human suffering, disability and disorientation, including advanced ageing and dementia.[8]

There is no doubt (though it is under-recognised) that the two disciples on the road to Emmaus are suffering, fleeing a place of trauma and continuing perceived danger, and deeply disoriented (vv. 17, 21). A child once advanced the theory that Mary Magdalene did not recognise the risen Christ because her eyes were too full of tears to see properly. Perhaps this is also relevant to this story.

In the Bible, thin places are often marked by the presence of angels. Luke's gospel actually opens with an encounter with an angel in a thin place – the temple (interestingly by a male priest who is unable to tell what he has seen) and it ends with an encounter with angels in a thin place – the tomb (by women who do tell what they have seen but are not believed by men). Both texts use the word *optasia* (vision) for these encounters.

The two disciples have all the perceptual building blocks in place but cannot form a percept – see what is front of their eyes - until they enter their own thin place, or more correctly as Jesus draws near and makes it a thin place. The text tells us that the two are 'held' or 'kept' from recognising Jesus perhaps, as already suggested, by their grief; perhaps by their attempts to cope with it by talking it through; perhaps by the obvious fact that Jesus is dead so he is the last person you would expect to see.

But Jesus is also presented as an ordinary stranger who is only recognisable in hindsight by the impact that his joining up of scripture with their recent experience had on their burning hearts. There is an opportunity here to explore end of life as providing the wisdom of hindsight. The

extract from a Holy Week address below describes this process:

This fitting of things together to make sense is something we do increasingly as we approach the end of our lives. Indeed, some things only make sense with the hindsight of years. In the last week of his life, an elderly friend told me a story. When he was engaged to be married, he and his fiancée searched in vain for somewhere to live. It was just after World War II and, like today, there was a shortage of affordable rental accommodation. It looked very much as if they were going to have to begin their married life living with his parents. Then, a few days before the wedding, a large flat became available at a reasonable rent. Over the years, my friend and his wife had often said to each other that this had been like a wonderful miracle. But in his last days, he returned to this part of his life and he remembered something odd; he had a flashbulb memory of his aunt whispering conspiratorially to his mother-in-law shortly before the flat became available. This aunt was wealthy and had contacts in the property business. Over 60 years after the original incident, he realised that she must have slipped someone a financial sweetener to secure the flat for him. He had always thought this aunt rather cold and aloof; in his last days, he was filled with gratitude at her love and care for him and his new bride. He felt compelled to tell me the story 'in remembrance of her' (Mark 14:9).

There is here a kind of unlocking of the imagination that enables the consideration of previously unthought of possibilities – possibilities to do with this earthly life (the insight that there is more to people and situations than meets the eye) and of God's glory that is both profoundly different from and far greater than we could have hoped or imagined. This unlocking of the imagination is a mark of the resurrection life; when we 'get it' we are –as it were – raised with Christ.

Our encounters in thin places are transitory, yet we have a desire to hold on to them. The disciples here urge the stranger to stay longer and, just when they realise who he is, he has gone. Something similar happens at the transfiguration – another 'vision' – where Peter tries to build 'dwelling places' for Jesus, Moses and Elijah (Matthew 17:4). Notice here the link to 'Moses and all the prophets' in the Emmaus story (v. 27). Notice also what it is that Jesus draws out of scripture – that his suffering was the threshold to his glory, his own 'thin place'.

Even though the encounter with Jesus is so fleeting these disciples are able to live in its light. They turn around and reattach themselves to the emerging church and they offer a 'bottom-up theology' based on their own first-hand experience that at once supports, complements and subverts the top-down pronouncements of the proto-magisterium on the lips of Peter.

This passage ends at an unusual point (v. 36) with the words 'Peace be with you.' For this is our ultimate desired destination; a place of deep peace and security in the presence of Jesus.

Growing: sermon starter

1 Corinthians 15:35–58: transformation of the body

Jeremy Brooks writes: In a sermon on growth, it seems strange that the key text appears to be about dying. Jesus' words in John 12:24–25 go to the heart of the matter. 'Unless a grain of wheat falls into the earth and dies, it remains just a single grain, but if it dies it bears much fruit'. Death is the pathway to life; spiritual growth comes not through insisting on living, but on embracing dying: then is the way open for there to be much fruit. Similarly, 1 Corinthians 15:35–58 seems wholly taken up with arguments about life after death and what that will look like: how does it speak to us whilst we are still living?

In order to understand that, I think we need to step back a little and consider the way of discipleship. Douglas Davies, in his study on *The Theology of Death* points out that Christianity is the most death-focused of all religions.[9] At our baptisms, we go down into the deep waters of death; at the Eucharist we are invited to remember and participate in the death of Christ. The most pressing call that Jesus makes on his disciples as he bids them come to follow him is to take up their cross – the only way to do that is to be nailed to it and die. And of course, through Christ's death and resurrection, comes our life.

Death in other words, within the Christian tradition, is not simply the event that takes place at the end of our lives: it is the gateway to fullness of life which takes place at our baptisms, and as disciples we are invited constantly to take the path of death in order to know life and growth. In that light, those words of Jesus in John 12 take on a different hue: they speak not just of his own forthcoming death, but point us to the way of discipleship.

The gospels are full of imagery of seeds being buried and growing. There are passages like Mark 4:32–34 where Jesus talks about a mustard seed as a tiny seed which is sown in the ground and becomes a great tree. Although we interpret Jesus' words in John 12 in an individual sense – they are about the individual death as the way of discipleship – Mark 4 has been used in a more corporate sense. Thus, the mustard seed is like the church which can grow and make a difference. However, Mark 4 also challenges our individual discipleship: if we want to show growth in our lives, will we be prepared to be like a seed that falls into the ground and dies before growth can come?

It is in this context that we can understand Paul's words in 1 Corinthians 15. It is a passionate discussion about what sort of life we have beyond the grave, but it makes no sense unless we can see that it is part of a continuum that includes our Christian discipleship before the grave. That is why Paul writes in the present tense in his second letter to the Corinthians that 'all of us *are being* transformed… from one degree of glory to another' (2 Corinthians 3:18).

In 1 Corinthians, Paul is at his most argumentative with those to whom he is writing. There are people in Corinth who say that truly spiritual people – the *pneumatikos* person – has put aside the body and such things are not important. They have scoffed at Paul's teaching that the body will be raised at the last day and caricatured it by painting pictures of resuscitated corpses. Bodies are only good for decay, they say: what matters is the disembodied soul which will live forever.

Paul argues strongly in this passage that the bodies we get at the resurrection are not disembodied souls, but neither are they revived corpses. He too uses the analogy of a seed that is planted in the ground in verse 37, but then the seed is clothed with a new body by God at the resurrection. The point that he makes is that what grows from the ground looks as different from the original seed as our resurrection bodies look to our earthly bodies but they are completely connected to one another. In verses 43 and 44, he highlights the differences between them but stresses the link too: 'it is sown in dishonour, it is raised in glory. It is sown in weakness, it is raised in power'.

I think these words have particular power for us as we get older. Young people's bodies are still considered beautiful and glorious and the ideal to try and keep. It is noticeable that a recent BBC series about old people was entitled 'How to stay young' rather than 'How to be old well'. Old age is seen as a problem, youth a gift. Most of this is because our attitudes to old age are negative because our physical bodies are in a time of decline.

So when Paul talks about our earthly bodies being perishable and weak, those of us who are older or living with a chronic health condition or disability know exactly what he means because we are living it out! However, we need not fear the decline of our bodies because transformation of our whole selves is also taking place. Just as there are inevitable physical losses to old age – and they will be different for different people – so we all have the potential for gain in other parts of our life. We have the potential for greater wisdom, we will have greater experience, many older people are far more accepting of social change than those many years younger. There is growth that comes with age as well as decline. Madeleine le Sueur, the American author who lived to be 96 said towards the end of her life 'I have become luminous with age'.

This is why Paul ends with verse 58, which seems slightly out of place in the rest of his argument: 'Be steadfast, immovable, always excelling in the work of the Lord, because you know that in the Lord your labour is not in vain'. We excel in the Lord's work when we follow the path of discipleship, which leads to growth and transformation.

In Christian theology, the daily death that we are called upon to accept in order to know daily transformation will ultimately result in physical death in order to know ultimate transformation. That is why the cross can be seen as the tree of life for us all.

Belonging: sermon starter

Matthew 6:25–30; 10:28–31: Maslow turned upside down

These two short extracts from Matthew's gospel are part of the teaching material that is also found in Luke but not in Mark (or John). There are a variety of views on the origin of this material but it is agreed that much of it is in the form of Jewish wisdom teaching. The reference to lilies (*krina*) in 6:28 conjures up strong associations with the Song of Songs (where they are mentioned six times) and, if this wasn't enough, immediately afterwards there is an explicit reference to Solomon, the archetypal wise man. All this alerts us to the fact that Jesus is talking about wisdom. The first passage is about life wisdom and the second passage is about death wisdom.

This is about growing up to be who we were meant to be. Scholars argue about whether the word translated 'hour' (v. 27) is actually a unit of length. But the ambiguity holds an important truth. Jesus is telling his listeners that they need to come to full maturity (Matthew 5:48), and this means both being riper in years and taller in stature.

What does this look like in practice? Fundamentally, it seems to involve getting one's priorities right. It's not that food and clothing are not good (this is made clear in verse 32) but that there is something even more important. This kind of wisdom inverts Abraham Maslow's famous hierarchy, which assumes that basic needs (for physiological sustenance and physical safety) have to be met before one is in a position to engage with higher needs for belonging and self-worth, which in their turn must be met before one has a chance to achieve self-actualisation.[10]

Jesus seems to be telling his hearers exactly the opposite: to go for the ultimate values embodied in the programme he calls the kingdom of God. If we do this we will find that these other needs will also be met. This is subversive wisdom.

Subversive wisdom makes us anxious because it goes against conventional norms; and anxiety means that we cannot pay full attention to what is really important. That is why Jesus warns against worry and fear. Interestingly, his argument is centred on one of Maslow's needs: self-worth. We do not need to be afraid because we are worth something; we matter. This doesn't depend on anything that we do. We matter because everything in creation matters to God and is under his sovereign authority; even little birds that you can buy two-a-penny; even ephemeral wild flowers. God is seen to have taken great trouble in creating these things (another theme from the Hebrew wisdom literature), endowing them with beauty and providing them with sustenance as part of the natural order. This is equally true of humanity, the crown of creation, but even more so because we have been bought at great cost (1 Corinthians 6:20). God thought we were worth that.

The reference to the hairs of our heads in 6:30 seems to indicate that God is focused on the individual. He has created each flower, each bird, each person, each hair. He has made us each unique (Psalm 139:13–16), and that seems to be part of the reason that we are so precious to him. Yet Jesus talks about lilies and birds in the plural, and all the 'yous' in these passages are Greek plurals. Just as each flower has its place in the ecosystem that is the meadow, and each bird has its place in the flock, so we each have our unique place as a worker for the kingdom of God, our unique place as a member of the body of Christ, our unique place in the cosmos. And here we are back with Maslow, who identifies 'belonging' as a major human need, closely related to love. God shows his love for us by coming to pitch his tent among us and redeeming us through his death; but he also shows it by drawing us into a community whose members are enough like us to give us a sense of solidarity, yet different enough from us that we can find our unique place, and with it, dignity.

This message of the kingdom as an inverted Maslow's triangle is important for all people, but it is a particularly powerful message for those who are in situations of poverty, chronic sickness, political oppression, exploitation and persecution without hope of human intervention (Jesus' original audience). It tells us that we can still grow up into self-actualisation – a life full of dignity and meaning – even if many of our basic needs have not been met. And of course this is the story of so many of the great saints, creative geniuses and political reformers of history: we can triumph over our circumstances and be liberated from them. This is perhaps what Jesus is emphasising in 6:28; if others deprive us of food, clothing, safety, love, belonging and self-worth, we need not despair because we belong to Christ, who gives us all.

And if we are fortunate enough to have most of these material and social blessings, like many in the developed west, we do not need to be afraid of losing them. We are freed from lives dominated by anxiety for the future and, above all, by the threat of death. Once we grasp this deep truth about the kingdom we no longer live under death's dominion. Living out this reality means that we cannot be forced to do anything because the ultimate sanction – fear – has been removed. We are no longer slaves, but we give of ourselves freely (Matthew 5:39–41; John 10:18), and we do this not on our own but as salt and yeast in company with other kingdom people. Here the economy of the kingdom flies in the face of conventional logic; these free acts of self-giving don't, as we might expect, serve to perpetuate the unjust structures of this world, but – as Mary proclaims in the Magnificat – to challenge, break down and ultimately transform them.

Hoping: sermon starter

Romans 8:18–39: dwelling in suffering, yearning and hope

Jeremy Brooks writes: It is perhaps stating the obvious to say that the context of our lives deeply affects the ways in which we encounter scripture. Sometimes familiar bits of scripture accompany us though rites of passage or moments of significance, providing a continuity and a clarity to our journey with God. On other occasions, a particular experience may give us fresh eyes or a new encounter with God through the Bible, lending new insight into the familiar or drawing the less familiar into clearer view.

Liturgical time can make a difference too, and this part of Romans 8 will find astonishingly different resonances with different liturgical seasons. Read it in Advent, and the focus of the passage is immediately drawn to the 'eager longing for the revealing of the children of God' (v. 21), as we await the coming of the Christ-child and our Lord's return. Read it again at Christmas, and the groaning in labour pains of creation (v. 22) makes connections with Mary's own groaning as her body delivers the glory of God incarnate. Read the passage in Lent and Passiontide, however, and it's verse 18 which really sets the tone for the season, as present suffering is placed in the context of future glory. If we read in Easter, then the declaration that 'all things work together for good for those who love God' (v. 28) is understood as a hope which is based on the resurrection, rather than a vague reassurance sometime in the future. Reading the passage in that long stretch of Sundays after Trinity, and the solidarity with the renewal and redemption of all creation might be what catches our eye.

As it happens, we encounter this section (split up) twice in the Sunday lectionary readings, and both times on or in the season of Pentecost. It's natural at this point to focus on the wider context of the first two thirds of the chapter, which describe in detail the work of the Spirit in the hearts of believers and in the whole created order, and culminating in this outpouring of hope.

Having said all that, there is one day in the year when I think the whole momentum of this passage takes a very significant meaning. That day is Holy Saturday, the time between crucifixion and resurrection. It may be one day in the calendar, but it's always worth remembering that for anyone in our care facing a terminal diagnosis, a family member slipping further into the clutches of dementia, the time between a death and a funeral, or proximity to an anniversary of a loved one's passing, Holy Saturday may be any day in the year. It's the day when Jesus is out of sight and out of reach, when darkness still covers the earth, and faced with despair, all we can do is wait. It's a day which perhaps more than any other demands our deep theological exploration and pastoral sensitivity in equal measure.

On Holy Saturday we are acutely aware that Christ has shared in our suffering, and that following a call which demands we take up our own crosses will inevitably and inexorably lead us to the same place. In this context, we might see in verses 18–25 four sentences which set out the three themes that Paul weaves together: suffering, yearning and hoping; a mirror of the Triduum. Just as Christ shows solidarity in our pain, so we are bound up with the suffering and the redemption of the whole creation.

There is no denial of the impact of suffering here. Paul's own life was spent first inflicting on others the suffering entailed in Christian discipleship, and then taking that same suffering upon himself. He knew first-hand what the consequences of this way of life would be. Looking ahead in the chapter (v. 35), Paul explicitly names the suffering he has experienced for the sake of the gospel. So when he considers the 'sufferings of this present time' (v. 18), and the whole creation's 'bondage to decay' (v. 21), these are not trivial difficulties, but matters of life and death.

Perhaps because giving birth to new life is a dangerous and life-threatening act, Paul uses birth as an analogy for the suffering and the renewal of creation. I wonder if there is a more succinct description of labour than this: 'I consider that the sufferings of this present time are not worth comparing with the glory about to be revealed to us' (v. 18)? And verse 19 also picks up on the anticipation of creation holding its breath with eager longing for the revealing of the children of God, much like those final stages of a pregnancy. It's language that has deliberate echoes of the original moments of creation; before there was anything else, there was simply God. And so, womblike, God has to make space within Godself for the creation simply to have a space to exist. As life is brought into existence, it is through the breaking of waters that chaos gradually transforms itself into order, and all is declared good.

That the total goodness does not last is a human legacy. 'Cursed is the ground because of you' hear Eve and Adam (Genesis 3:17).

All creation is damaged by the carelessness of humankind, as it continues to be. 'For the creation was subjected to futility, not of its own will' (v. 20) is how Paul puts it. Creation waits to 'obtain the freedom of the glory of the children of God' (v. 21), but in the meantime this is a painful and not a passive waiting. It's tempting when we encounter this suffering in the text to want to skip over it and get straight to the reassurance. But it would be a mistake not to dwell a little longer in this time before everything is made a new creation.

The language of labour pains is then used to describe the groaning that both creation and those who have received the Spirit endure as they are simultaneously made anew and adopted. This is the moment that suffering changes to yearning. Much like labour, this is a purposeful groaning which aches and strains for the first glimpses of new life. Our own yearning for all to be made well is taken up by the Spirit on our behalf (vv. 23, 26–28). To remain with the birthing image, it acts like a doula (birth partner) – reminding us that whatever our pain and whatever our longing, we are not alone. Even in the most difficult and trying of places, God is still somehow with us. Not for nothing has there been a tradition that Holy Saturday is the day in the calendar when Jesus descends to harrow hell. In the one place that God should not be, the work of redemption is already beginning.

'Everything will all be alright in the end. And if it's not alright, it's not yet the end.' So says the somewhat unlikely theologian Sonny Kapoor in the 2011 film *The Best Exotic Marigold Hotel*. Just as suffering is transformed to yearning, so is yearning transformed into hoping. 'For in hope we were saved' (v. 24) writes Paul. This is not the end of the story. Easter Sunday will bring about the renewal of all things, but we are not quite there yet. Indeed 'we hope for what we do not see' (v. 25). It may take a while to get there, and we may need to spend time alongside those who are experiencing suffering and yearning, but we do not lose sight of the hope that Paul reaches – 'All things work together for good for those who love God' (v. 28). We who witness to this hope are the first-fruits of this promise.

There is an awkward addendum that must be addressed at the end of this densely packed outpouring. The final question we're left with from this passage is this – is this hope for everyone? At first glance, the appearance of the word 'predestined' in the final couple of verses might indicate otherwise. I find Tom Wright's thoughts on verse 30, and the language of predestined, called, justified and glorified, a helpful clarification here.

> *That is a sharp, close-up, compressed telling of Israel as the chosen people, whose identity and destiny is then brought into sharp focus on Jesus (and in a sense Jesus is the one chosen one)... That identity is then shared with all those who are in Christ.*[11]

The answer to the question then is that hope is for everyone who is in Christ. Jesus is the culmination of Israel's story, and the means by which we come to share in their calling as God's people. Through him we are justified, and by joining with him as people of the resurrection we are glorified.

Let us not forget the pastoral importance here. Holy Saturday requires us to wait for the transforming that God will bring through the resurrection of Jesus. But it also requires us be entirely present in the moment of the pain of absence – not always knowing how to pray and relying on the Spirit to groan deeply on our behalf. Good Friday feels like the day when we have abandoned God; Holy Saturday feels like the day when God has abandoned us. Even in this moment though, the Spirit still intercedes for us, and we are called to painful, patient, purposeful hope.

Finally then, this passage reminds us that hope is what sustains all of creation within God's story. The great hope of Easter transforms our perspective on the spoiling of creation, the waywardness of a people, the violence of a crucifixion and the suffering of the present time. It reminds us that God always finds a way to bring beauty out of brokenness, closeness out of abandonment, joy out of despair, until the creation once again reveals the full glory of its creator.

Bible studies

Loving: Bible study

Living as a community of love

The themes to be explored in this study are the way that living as a community of love involves sacrifice and a dying to self. Love is a concept which all of us are familiar with and happy to use, but which also has such a vast variety of meanings and applications that it can sometimes seem a bland or vacuous concept. The love of God is explored throughout the Bible in a number of ways, and exploring these themes may help tie down what is unique and important about what Christians have to say on the subject.

Before reading the Bible passage(s), your group may find it helpful to look at this painting by Agnolo Bronzino, called *The Madonna and Child with Saints*, which dates from 1540:

nationalgallery.org.uk/paintings/bronzino-the-madonna-and-child-with-saints

Notes on the painting

> This is a late Renaissance work, probably painted at the Medici court in Florence. The garland of flowers playfully carried by one of the children is a symbol of that city, and is one of several symbols in the painting. The young woman is Mary and the child on her lap with the garland is the infant Jesus. The child leaning against her is the infant John the Baptist; he is wearing a cloak of animal skins and carries a baptismal bowl. The older woman may be his mother, Elizabeth, or possibly St Anne (Mary's mother according to tradition.)
>
> John is usually depicted carrying a reed cross (a reference to Matthew 11:7), but in this picture Jesus has playfully snatched it from him. In doing this he points forward to his own sacrificial death.
>
> But the artist has positioned the cross (which also looks like a sword) carefully; it points downwards towards Mary's heart. Thus it foreshadows the pain she will experience as her son is taken from her (Luke 2:35), and is a mark of her own sacrificial love.
>
> The picture is full of maternal care and intimacy. Three of the characters seem to be smiling, but Mary's appears to be pondering, perhaps on the fact that grief is the price we pay for love.

Opening questions

> Can you identify the characters in the painting?
>
> What do the directions of gaze of the different characters communicate to you?
>
> Does this painting have something to say about the love between generations?

Bible passage: 1 Corinthians 13:1–8

> *If I speak in the tongues of humans and of angels, but do not have love, I am a noisy gong or a clanging cymbal. And if I have prophetic powers and understand all mysteries and all knowledge and if I have all faith so as to remove mountains but do not have love, I am nothing. If I give away all my possessions, and if I hand over my body so that I may boast, but do not have love, I gain nothing. Love is patient; love is kind; love is not envious or boastful or arrogant or rude. It does not insist on its own way; it is not irritable; it keeps no record of wrongs; it does not rejoice in wrongdoing but rejoices in the truth. It bears all things, believes all things, hopes all things, endures all things. Love never ends.*

Questions

> Paul defines love both by what it is and what it isn't. Could anything be added to his list of either? How is the example of God's love in Jesus expressed positively and/or negatively?
>
> How do we identify love when we listen to others? What helps us to distinguish the tongues of angels from a clanging cymbal?
>
> Love 'bears all things, believes all things, hopes all things, endures all things'. How does loving affect our experience of bearing, believing, hoping or enduring?
>
> 1 Corinthians is written to a community, and this expression of love is to be taken immediately in the context of what comes before it, where Paul describes the body of Christ as having many parts. Is it easier to offer the love described here, or to be a recipient of it?
>
> How does love relate to the different forms of power we encounter here?

Wider questions

What part does love have to play when we near the end of our lives?

The passage later concludes with these words 'And now faith, hope, and love remain, these three, and the greatest of these is love.' Why might the greatest be love? How does love make sense of faith and hope?

How does a Christian account of love differ from a secular one?

Additional passages

Here are four passages in addition to the main one above. You could have a one-off study on a single passage, a series using all five passages, or break up a larger group into small subgroups to look at one passage each and then come back to share common themes.

Psalm 23

What reasons can you give for why this passage is so familiar to so many people?

The psalm names the presence of God with us in both times of contentedness and times of trouble. Which of these experiences has brought you especially close to God?

How can we resist the urge to fix problems at the expense of faithful presence with those in the 'darkest valley'?

There are resonances of Jesus' final few days with his disciples in verse 5. Why might these become especially important with those who are near to death?

John 13:1–17, 31–35; 15:12–13

'By this everyone will know that you are my disciples'. How could being a community of love be an outward-facing venture, as well as an internal intention for a group? Does one always risk becoming the other?

Some commentators have seen the washing of feet as a preparation for dying, and Jesus' words to Peter about washing the whole body as about baptism. What is the relationship between baptism and death? What parallels could be drawn between Jesus' baptism and his death?

> How do Jesus' actions here makes sense of Mary anointing Jesus' feet in John 12, or is it the other way around? What do the two events imply about the cost of love?
>
> Which sentence in this passage do you find to be the most challenging, and which the most comforting? Why?

Song of Songs 8:1–7

> Do you find the poetic expressions of love more or less helpful that other forms of biblical writing (for example, Paul's letters)?
>
> This passage uses labour as a frequent image. How does it inform the idea of being born again?
>
> Which other parts of scripture resonate with the declaration that water cannot quench love, or floods drown it?

1 John 4:7–21

> Verses 9–10 tell of how God's love is revealed to God's creation. Can that revelation of love be imitated, or is the way we reveal God's love different?
>
> Reading verse 18, what do you think the relationship between love and discipline is?
>
> The final couple of verses seem to imply that loving our brothers and sisters comes as a result of seeing God's love within them first. Where or when do you find it most difficult to see love? What can blind love from sight?

Letting go: Bible study

Sit lightly to things

The theme to be explored in this study is the biblical call to sit lightly to things that we might naturally wish to grasp in an attempt to give ourselves a sense of stability and security, or legacy and immortality. This requires us to get our priorities straight and, in the light of Christ and his kingdom, to focus on what is essential at any one time.

Before reading the Bible passage(s), your group may find it helpful to look at a painting by J.M.W. Turner, called *The Fighting Temeraire*, which dates from 1839.

nationalgallery.org.uk/paintings/joseph-mallord-william-turner-the-fighting-temeraire

Notes on the painting

> Turner painted this in the midst of what may have been depression or a very long and complicated bereavement following the death of his father, his main close confidant, in 1829.
>
> Its subject is a 98-gun naval warship that had been launched in 1798 and went on to play a key role in the Battle of Trafalgar, going into action astern of *HMS Victory*. She went into retirement in Plymouth in 1812, had an afterlife as a prison ship, but was eventually broken up in 1838.
>
> The painting depicts a steam-powered tug towing the magnificent but now elderly and rather ghostly looking ship to her final destination. The ship that had once been part of a sailing fleet that ruled the waves is now obsolete in a new age of steam power and industrialisation, already fading in memory as she is in the picture.
>
> She is being led 'where you do not wish to go' (John 21:18)

Opening questions

> Is this sunrise or sunset?
>
> What is the mood of the painting?
>
> How does it make you feel?

Bible passage: John 21:1–19

After these things Jesus showed himself again to the disciples by the Sea of Tiberias, and he showed himself in this way. Gathered there together were Simon Peter, Thomas called the Twin, Nathanael of Cana in Galilee, the sons of Zebedee, and two others of his disciples. Simon Peter said to them, 'I am going fishing.' They said to him, 'We will go with you.' They went out and got into the boat, but that night they caught nothing.

Just after daybreak, Jesus stood on the beach, but the disciples did not know that it was Jesus. Jesus said to them, 'Children, you have no fish, have you?' They answered him, 'No.' He said to them, 'Cast the net to the right side of the boat, and you will find some.' So they cast it, and now they were not able to haul it in because there were so many fish. That disciple whom Jesus loved said to Peter, 'It is the Lord!' When Simon Peter heard that it was the Lord, he put on his outer garment, for he had taken it off, and jumped into the sea. But the other disciples came in the boat, dragging the net full of fish, for they were not far from the land, only about a hundred yards off.

When they had gone ashore, they saw a charcoal fire there, with fish on it, and bread. Jesus said to them, 'Bring some of the fish that you have just caught.' So Simon Peter went aboard and hauled the net ashore, full of large fish, a hundred fifty-three of them, and though there were so many, the net was not torn. Jesus said to them, 'Come and have breakfast.' Now none of the disciples dared to ask him, 'Who are you?' because they knew it was the Lord. Jesus came and took the bread and gave it to them and did the same with the fish. This was now the third time that Jesus appeared to the disciples after he was raised from the dead.

When they had finished breakfast, Jesus said to Simon Peter, 'Simon son of John, do you love me more than these?' He said to him, 'Yes, Lord; you know that I love you.' Jesus said to him, 'Feed my lambs.' A second time he said to him, 'Simon son of John, do you love me?' He said to him, 'Yes, Lord; you know that I love you.' Jesus said to him, 'Tend my sheep.' He said to him the third time, 'Simon son of John, do you love me?' Peter felt hurt because he said to him the third time, 'Do you love me?' And he said to him, 'Lord, you know everything; you know that I love you.' Jesus said to him, 'Feed my sheep. Very truly, I tell you, when you were younger, you used to fasten your own belt and to go wherever you wished. But when you grow old, you will stretch out your hands, and someone else will fasten a belt around you and take you where you do not wish to go.' (He said this to indicate the kind of death by which he would glorify God.) After this he said to him, 'Follow me.'

Questions

What is behind Peter's decision to go fishing (v. 3)?

The whole story points back to earlier events. How many can you identify?

Why do you think John draws out these earlier connections?

What is Peter being asked to let go of here? What is driving him forward (see John 6:66–69)?

Jesus himself is letting go here. What does he have to say goodbye to and how does he do this?

What can this passage tell us about making good endings?

Wider questions

How do we help people make transitions, especially those that involve laying down a responsibility in our churches? Should we challenge the idea of 'jobs for life' in the culture of many congregations?

How do we make a good transition from old ways of doing things to ways that are more suitable for our time without doing violence to the wisdom and beauty of the past?

How can we challenge the instinct that retirement is simply the prelude (however extended) to a final journey?

Additional passages

Here are four passages in addition to the main one above. You could have a one-off study on a single passage, a series using all five passages, or break up a larger group into small subgroups to look at one passage each and then come back to share common themes.

Philippians 2:5–8

In this passage Paul is exhorting his readers to imitate Jesus in his act of letting go of his entitlement and status and taking on the lowliest of human forms. How did Jesus show this in his life? How did he show it in his death? How are the two connected?

Unlike Jesus, we are not divine. What are we asked to let go of?

What are the things that are most difficult for you to let go of? What does that tell you about yourself?

In talking of the 'mind' Paul seems to be saying that our attitude is at least as much as our behaviour. How might a 'letting go' attitude be life-giving for us?

Mark 1:16–20; 8:34–37

What do these fishermen leave behind and what do they take with them when Jesus calls them?

Taking up one's cross might mean physical martyrdom, but it might be expressed in losses in other aspects of life. What might this look like? Can you make sense of your own Christian journey as laying things down in order to take up the cross?

The Greek word translated 'life' here (*psuchē*) can also be translated 'self' or 'soul'. What does it mean to lose your soul in order to gain it? Does the idea of a false self (or persona) versus a true self help?

John 14:16–19; 16:5–12

These passages are a small part of Jesus' long goodbye to his disciples during the last supper. He is helping his followers to let go of him. How does he do this?

The passages are full of emotion that goes beyond the surface meanings of the words. What feelings can you detect in them? How do they make you feel?

Jesus talks of the Holy Spirit as the 'paraclete', translated here as 'advocate' but in some other versions as 'comforter'. These words capture different aspects of the Spirit's role: to help us see meaning and truth in the dark events of the death of Jesus and to assure as that we are not alone. How do these two themes relate to your experience of bereavement?

Luke 12:16–23

What do you think the rich fool is trying to protect himself from?

Do you think this passage is about material acquisitiveness or does it also have something to say about bolstering self-worth through building up achievements or marks of status?

This is a story about an individual who seems to be cut off from others (v. 20 emphasises this). What does this have to tell us about the need for interconnectedness if we are truly to live? Could we apply this to nations as well as to individuals?

Seeing: Bible study

The veiling and unveiling of reality

The theme to be explored in this study is the veiling and unveiling of reality. Catching glimpses of a heavenly perspective in epiphany moments is something that can happen at any time in the Christian journey, but it seems to be especially intense at life-and-death events such as childbirth or as earthly life draws to its close.

Before reading the Bible passage(s) your group may find it helpful to look at this painting by Michelangelo Merisi da Caravaggio, called *The Supper at Emmaus*, which dates from 1601. The painting captures a particular moment in the Road to Emmaus story from Luke 24 – the moment of recognition.

nationalgallery.org.uk/paintings/michelangelo-merisi-da-caravaggio-the-supper-at-emmaus

Notes on the painting

> Caravaggio (unlike his followers) never shows his light source. The light source is to the left and fore of the frame. This cleverly throws the shadow of the innkeeper behind Jesus, perhaps suggesting that Jesus is the true host (even though he is a guest at the inn presumably paid for by the disciples).
>
> The innkeeper keeps his hat on in the presence of Jesus and does not share the astonishment of the disciples. This seems to indicate that he doesn't share in their epiphany.
>
> Jesus is depicted with a face that was unconventional for depictions of Christ the time and drew some criticism. Is Caravaggio trying to emphasise that Jesus is a stranger who goes unrecognised?
>
> The bowl of fruit in the foreground may symbolise the fruit of the Spirit, specifically the pomegranate may represent the church. But also note that the shadow it casts is that of a fish. This may also represent the church or it may point to later in the story when Jesus eats a piece of grilled fish in the presence of his disciples (Luke 24:41–43), which itself refers back to the feeding of the multitudes.
>
> The cockle shell worn by one of the men indicates that he stands for all Christ's pilgrim people, each on their own journey.
>
> The posture of the disciples communicate the suddenness of the revelation, and the way perspective is used both makes them appear to come out of the canvas and to draw us in.

Opening questions

> How would you describe the mood of the painting?
>
> How does it make you feel?
>
> Caravaggio has depicted the events in his own time and culture. What might it look like in our locality today?

Bible passage: Luke 24:28–31

> *As they came near the village to which they were going, [Jesus] walked ahead as if he were going on. But they urged him strongly, saying, 'Stay with us, because it is almost evening and the day is now nearly over.' So he went in to stay with them. When he was at the table with them, he took bread, blessed and broke it, and gave it to them. Then their eyes were opened, and they recognised him; and he vanished from their sight.*

Questions

> The epiphany happens at the end of the day. Does this have something to say about insights achieved towards the end of life?
>
> An ordinary act in an ordinary setting is transfigured. Have you ever experienced 'heaven in ordinary'?
>
> The opening of the disciples' eyes is a kind of remembering – a recognition. It's a joining up of the present with the past. Is this true of your moments of insight? Does it mean that later life is a time when such insights are likely to be more frequent and intense?

Wider questions

> Our glimpses of heaven in this life are infused with mystery but also sometimes intimacy. How can we speak of them? Is it easier to communicate them through creative media such as poetry, visual art or music? Dare we speak of such things or are we too embarrassed?
>
> How do we receive heavenly visions from 'implausible' witnesses, for example children, people with dementia, people with mental health conditions, people who are dying? (Look at Acts 2:17).

Additional passages

Here are four passages in addition to the main one above. You could have a one-off study on a single passage, a series using all five passages, or break up a larger group into small subgroups to look at one passage each and then come back to share common themes.

John 1:45–51

How many times is seeing mentioned in this passage? Who does the seeing in this passage?

The first words that Jesus speaks in John's gospel are 'What are you looking for?' (John 1:38). What are his last two words (John 21:22)?

Nathanael achieves his insight only when he sets his human preconceptions aside. What leads him to do this?

Jesus suggests (alluding to Genesis 28:10–12) that true seeing involves access to a 'higher' vision? How is this access achieved?

Why are the angels important? Angels and other winged creatures are often associated with death in people's minds; why might this be?

Matthew 16:13–23

Jesus is not interested in second-hand opinions on the part of the disciples. Why do you think this is and how does this connect with 'seeing'?

Peter seems unable to hold on to his higher vision and instead has difficulty setting his human preconceptions aside. (Nathanael's problem is that Jesus comes from the wrong side of the tracks; Peter's problem is the way of the cross). What might it mean for us to set our preconceptions aside?

Colossians 3:1–2

Here we again have reference to a higher vision; what are 'the things that are above' and 'the things that are on earth? (You may want to look at the rest of Colossians 3).

This passage mentions death, but who exactly has died and what does it mean?

1 Corinthians 13:9–12

Here, instead of a higher vision, Paul talks of an ultimate (and indeed intimate) vision. This vision will be achieved 'then.' When is 'then'?

What do Paul and Nathanael have in common?

How do we get through life until 'then' if we can only see dimly – as it were – in a blurred first-century looking glass? The next verse (1 Corinthians 13:13) may help here.

Growing: Bible study

Old age and dying as a time of growth

The theme to be explored in this study is that of old age and dying as a time of growth towards our ultimate reality which we know finally after death. In every day life, we know that the things that could tear us down – our disappointments, the sufferings we endure – can have the opposite effect and make us stronger. At the heart of the Christian faith is that it's what appears to be ultimate defeat and failure in death which is the pathway to the ultimate growth and life. It seems nonsensical to say that the journey towards death is about growing. Our instincts tell us it's more about diminishment. Yet there is much in the Bible that turns our traditional wisdom on its head and reminds us that God's way of looking at the world is completely different to our own.

Before reading the Bible passage(s) your group may find it helpful to look at this artwork by Edward Burne-Jones, called *Tree of Life*, which dates from 1888.

collections.vam.ac.uk/item/O88844/
tree-of-life-design-burne-jones-edward

Notes on the artwork

> This is a mosaic ceiling from the American Episcopal Church in Rome, St Paul-Within-the-Walls.
>
> It shows not Mary and John standing at the cross, but Adam and Eve by the tree of life.
>
> There are sheaves of corn growing abundantly in place of the curse that God gives Adam in Genesis 3:19 where Adam is forced to bring forth bread by the sweat of his brow. Briar thorns may still be drawn on Eve's side to represent her state of sin, but the eye is drawn much more to the lilies, the symbol of purity.
>
> Cain and Abel are represented not as murderous brother and victim, but as two babies, shown in innocence with the opportunity for growth.
>
> The Latin inscription means: 'You shall have affliction in the world, but have faith, for I have overcome the world'.

Opening questions

> Does it speak to you of life or of death?
>
> Do you find it threatening or welcoming? Why?
>
> What symbols and figures stand out to you? Why are they there?

Living well in the light of mortality

Bible passage: 1 Corinthians 15:35–58

But someone will ask, 'How are the dead raised? With what kind of body do they come?' Fool! What you sow does not come to life unless it dies. And as for what you sow, you do not sow the body that is to be but a bare seed, perhaps of wheat or of some other grain. But God gives it a body as he has chosen and to each kind of seed its own body. Not all flesh is alike, but there is one flesh for humans, another for animals, another for birds, and another for fish. There are both heavenly bodies and earthly bodies, but the glory of the heavenly is one thing, and that of the earthly is another. There is one glory of the sun and another glory of the moon and another glory of the stars; indeed, star differs from star in glory.

So it is with the resurrection of the dead. What is sown is perishable; what is raised is imperishable. It is sown in dishonor; it is raised in glory. It is sown in weakness; it is raised in power. It is sown a physical body; it is raised a spiritual body. If there is a physical body, there is also a spiritual body. Thus it is written, 'The first man, Adam, became a living being'; the last Adam became a life-giving spirit. But it is not the spiritual that is first but the physical and then the spiritual. The first man was from the earth, made of dust; the second man is from heaven. As one of dust, so are those who are of the dust, and as one of heaven, so are those who are of heaven. Just as we have borne the image of the one of dust, we will also bear the image of the one of heaven.

What I am saying, brothers and sisters, is this: flesh and blood cannot inherit the kingdom of God, nor does the perishable inherit the imperishable. Look, I will tell you a mystery! We will not all die, but we will all be changed, in a moment, in the twinkling of an eye, at the last trumpet. For the trumpet will sound, and the dead will be raised imperishable, and we will be changed. For this perishable body must put on imperishability, and this mortal body must put on immortality. When this perishable body puts on imperishability and this mortal body puts on immortality, then the saying that is written will be fulfilled: 'Death has been swallowed up in victory. Where, O death, is your victory? Where, O death, is your sting?' The sting of death is sin, and the power of sin is the law. But thanks be to God, who gives us the victory through our Lord Jesus Christ. Therefore, my beloved brothers and sisters, be steadfast, immovable, always excelling in the work of the Lord because you know that in the Lord your labor is not in vain.

Questions

Paul confronts the question of what will our existence be like after our deaths. How do you imagine it to be? What is Paul's answer to the Corinthians?

How does Paul use imagery from nature to explain what happens to us at death? Do you find this helpful?

What is the difference between a physical body and a spiritual body?

> What links and connections does Paul make between our bodies now and our bodies after death?
>
> Paul finishes his passage with a great cry of victory over death. How do you feel about dying? Take time to think through your own attitude to dying – either in silence, or you may feel able to share with the group how you feel. What are those things that scare or concern you? What is it that holds no fear at all?

Wider questions

> Why does Jesus use so many parables from nature and about growing in his teaching?
>
> How has your attitude to nature changed through your life? Since your childhood? Since you were a younger adult?
>
> Where do you see God in nature? Or do you find it easier to see him at work outside of nature?
>
> How do we fit into nature's plan of living and growing?

Additional passages

Here are four passages in addition to the main one above. You could have a one-off study on a single passage, a series using all five passages, or break up a larger group into small subgroups to look at one passage each and then come back to share common themes.

> #### John 12:20–28
>
> > What is the analogy that Jesus is drawing out between Christian discipleship and nature? Does this take on particular relevance as we get older or is it true at all times of our lives?
> >
> > Why does Jesus answer Philip and Andrew as he does? What do you think the Greeks at the festival would have made of the answer?
> >
> > Jesus appears to be talking of his own death. How do these words connect with our lives?
> >
> > Do you think the idea of a single grain of wheat can be applied as a metaphor to a community as well as an individual? What might it mean for your church community?

John 15:1–8; Mark 4:30–32

What does pruning have to do with growing?

Is Jesus talking about individual disciples here or a community? Do the words make sense to both? If so, how does pruning take place in your life as you get older?

Can you think of a local or national example of a Christian endeavour that began small and has grown into a big network? Share examples with each other.

How can you as an individual make a difference?

2 Corinthians 3:17–18

Imagine that the unveiled faces of which Paul speaks are like sunflower heads turned towards the light. Does this image ring true of certain Christians that you know as they have grown and matured in their faith? What is it about them that makes you think they are being transformed 'from one degree of glory to another'?

John 20:24–29

As you get older, are you more or less insistent on the need for physical proof for things?

Does Thomas show more or less faith than the other disciples in his response to Jesus compared to the others? Why is this?

Thomas is always called 'Doubting'. Is doubt connected in your mind with faith or a lack of it? Is doubt or faith related to at all to growing with age?

Belonging: Bible study

Our attachment to people and places

The theme to be explored in this study is the way our need for attachment to significant people and places seems to be connected with our need for self-worth; how death calls up terror in us because it seems to threaten both of these fundamental needs; and how the Bible deals with this head-on.

Before reading the Bible passage(s) your group may find it helpful to look at this painting by Stanley Spencer, called *Consider the Lilies*, which dates from 1939.

wikiart.org/en/stanley-spencer/christ-in-the-wilderness-consider-the-lilies

Notes on the painting

> The picture was painted at a time in Spencer's life when he was alone and disillusioned after a disastrous relationship had come to an end.
>
> He was trying to reconnect with his Christian faith. It's part of a series of eight paintings and 16 drawings entitled 'Christ in the Wilderness'. The wilderness perhaps refers more to Spencer than to Christ because the pictures are not all about Jesus' temptation in the desert.
>
> The series explores Christ's deep connection with nature. The recurring theme is that Jesus is alone, cut off from other human beings, but intimately connected with the natural world. Most of the paintings are about Jesus and animals (foxes, a hen, a scorpion, eagles), but this one is about flowers.
>
> Perhaps the most striking feature of the series is Jesus' size; he nearly fills the canvas. This may be an allusion to the fact that 'he fills all in all' (Ephesians 1:23). In comparison to his bulk, the lilies of the field are small.
>
> The lilies are actually daisies and larger than life. Spencer has located the Galilean lilies of the field in an English meadow.

Opening questions

> What is Spencer up to here?
>
> What is Jesus up to here?
>
> Does this depiction of Jesus feel familiar or strange to you?

Living well in the light of mortality

Bible passage: Matthew 6:25–29; 10:28–31

'Therefore I tell you, do not worry about your life, what you will eat or what you will drink, or about your body, what you will wear. Is not life more than food, and the body more than clothing? Look at the birds of the air; they neither sow nor reap nor gather into barns, and yet your heavenly Father feeds them. Are you not of more value than they? And can any of you by worrying add a single hour to your span of life? And why do you worry about clothing? Consider the lilies of the field, how they grow; they neither toil nor spin, yet I tell you, even Solomon in all his glory was not clothed like one of these. But if God so clothes the grass of the field, which is alive today and tomorrow is thrown into the oven, will he not much more clothe you – you of little faith? Therefore do not worry, saying, "What will we eat?" or "What will we drink?" or "What will we wear?" For it is the Gentiles who strive for all these things; and indeed your heavenly Father knows that you need all these things. But strive first for the kingdom of God and his righteousness, and all these things will be given to you as well. So do not worry about tomorrow, for tomorrow will bring worries of its own. Today's trouble is enough for today… Do not fear those who kill the body but cannot kill the soul; rather fear him who can destroy both soul and body in hell. Are not two sparrows sold for a penny? Yet not one of them will fall to the ground apart from your Father. And even the hairs of your head are all counted. So do not be afraid; you are of more value than many sparrows.'

Questions

Jesus talks about life in the first passage and about death in the second passage. In both he emphasises to his listeners that we have a high worth. He also talks about worry and fear. Psychologists have found fear of death to be closely linked to worry about self-worth. Why do you think this might be?

What do sowing and reaping and toiling and spinning have to do with self-worth? (Note that the first two were the conventional tasks of men and the second two the conventional tasks of women in Jesus' culture – he is addressing a mixed group.) What place does hard work have in a life well lived?

Jesus seems to be emphasising the power and authority of God as creator and sustainer of the natural living world right down to its smallest parts, but also as the one who has authority to judge all at the end of time. How might answering to this 'higher authority' affect the way we live our lives?

> Although it isn't that obvious at first, this passage is actually about being part of a family. Jesus isn't just using the birds and the flowers as a convenient metaphor; he is reminding his listeners that we are part of the natural order – we belong. On top of that he uses the phrases 'Your (plural) heavenly Father' in the first passage and 'your (plural) Father' in the second. Why do you think this is an important part of his argument?

Wider questions

> How might a sense of belonging help us to live and die well?
>
> People in residential care homes and hospitals who are nearing the end of life are also often cut off from nature. Yet we have seen that a connection with the natural world is part of what makes us feel human and less isolated. What can be done about this?
>
> How might the ideas explored in these studies inform the epidemic of loneliness in our society?

Additional passages

Here are four passages in addition to the main one above. You could have a one-off study on a single passage, a series using all five passages, or break up a larger group into small subgroups to look at one passage each and then come back to share common themes.

> **1 Corinthians 12**
>
>> Feeling that I am 'different' is often taken to imply feeling that I don't fit in. How does Paul challenge that idea in this passage?
>>
>> Have there been times in your life when you have felt desperate to fit in at the expense of being true to yourself? What have you learnt from those times?
>>
>> How can we help people find their place in church congregations or in the wider community so that they have a sense of belonging?
>>
>> Paul seems to be arguing that it is the Spirit that unites us. What does that mean in your experience?
>>
>> How can we resist the human desire to rank people in order of importance and treat them accordingly?
>
> **2 Corinthians 5**
>
>> This is a difficult passage. 'The earthly tent' is the stuff we have around us to stop us feeling exposed. What sort of stuff might this be? Is it our physical body or is it more than that – the stuff that gives us a sense of identity?

Paul seems to suggest that we may be reluctant to let go of our earthly tent, even though we know that there is a heavenly tent waiting for us, for fear of having to wait uncovered for it to materialise. He reassures us that for those who place their faith in Christ the transition from one to the other has already begun; we are being transformed. What evidence does he offer?

In your experience what does it look like when we invest too heavily and cling too hard to our 'earthly tent'?

We are used to thinking of mortal things being swallowed up by death. Paul talks of them being 'swallowed up by life' (v. 4). How do you understand this?

1 Thessalonians 4

What do you think Paul's main aim is in this passage? (the clues are in verses 13 and 18)

Find the phrases 'with him', 'together with them', 'with the Lord'. Why are these important?

How literally do you take Paul's description of the second coming? Do you find it encouraging or a bit weird? Or both?

Revelation 5

This is a wonderful vision of both the diversity and solidarity of God's creatures worshipping him forever in the heavenly places. Do you feel you want to be part of it? Have you ever glimpsed anything like this?

The creatures sing a new song of worship (v. 9). It's new because it is not to the Lion who conquers (v. 5) but to the Lamb who was slain (v. 6). Why is this so important?

The move from Lion to Lamb takes John by surprise, turning his expectations upside-down. Do you find God to be a God of surprises?

Hoping: Bible study

Perseverance in the light of present pain and future hope

The themes to be explored in this study are endurance and perseverance in the light of present pain and future hope. Hope is often discovered and strengthened in adversity, with the ultimate hope of eternal companionship with God the final answer to those parts of life which we find troubling and which induce anxiety. Rather than fixing problems, hope offers a perspective on how problems are experienced.

Before looking at the Bible passage your group may find it helpful to look at this Russian icon depicting the deposition of Jesus in the tomb, which dates from the fifteenth century.

webhome.auburn.edu/~mitrege/russian/icons/deposition.html

Notes on the painting

> The deposition of the body of Christ became a popular subject for religious art in the east and west in medieval times. There seems to have been a shift from celebrating the victory of Christ on the cross to focusing on his suffering and the anguish of those who lost him.
>
> This documentation of human grief and lament offers the bereaved viewer a compelling way of connecting with the story of Jesus, but there are also indications of hope.
>
> The inclusion of angels and a heavenly backdrop tells us that there is more to this story than meets the eye, that there is another perspective to be had and a better ending to be anticipated.
>
> The tender maternal embrace of a child wrapped in swaddling clothes about to be laid to rest hammers home the connections between birth and death, their liminal and mysterious nature, and the fact that one infuses the other with hope.

Opening questions

> What do the positions of the characters' hands convey to you?
>
> What are the angels doing?
>
> Why are the angels there at all?

Bible passage: Romans 8:22–39

We know that the whole creation has been groaning together as it suffers together the pains of labour, and not only the creation, but we ourselves, who have the first fruits of the Spirit, groan inwardly while we wait for adoption, the redemption of our bodies. For in hope we were saved. Now hope that is seen is not hope, for who hopes for what one already sees? But if we hope for what we do not see, we wait for it with patience.

Likewise the Spirit helps us in our weakness, for we do not know how to pray as we ought, but that very Spirit intercedes with groanings too deep for words. And God, who searches hearts, knows what is the mind of the Spirit, because the Spirit intercedes for the saints according to the will of God.

We know that all things work together for good for those who love God, who are called according to his purpose. For those whom he foreknew he also predestined to be conformed to the image of his Son, in order that he might be the firstborn within a large family. And those whom he predestined he also called, and those whom he called he also justified, and those whom he justified he also glorified.

What then are we to say about these things? If God is for us, who is against us? He who did not withhold his own Son but gave him up for all of us, how will he not with him also give us everything else? Who will bring any charge against God's elect? It is God who justifies. Who is to condemn? It is Christ who died, or rather, who was raised, who is also at the right hand of God, who also intercedes for us. Who will separate us from the love of Christ? Will affliction or distress or persecution or famine or nakedness or peril or sword? As it is written, 'For your sake we are being killed all day long; we are accounted as sheep to be slaughtered.' No, in all these things we are more than victorious through him who loved us. For I am convinced that neither death, nor life, nor angels, nor rulers, nor things present, nor things to come, nor powers, nor height, nor depth, nor anything else in all creation will be able to separate us from the love of God in Christ Jesus our Lord.

Questions

What is Paul hoping for?

How is hope connected with waiting?

What are the grounds for Paul's hope?

What is Paul doing as he weaves together words like 'groan', 'weakness', 'we are being killed', with 'glorified', 'know', 'convinced'? How does this mix connect with your experience of life?

Wider questions

> What is the relationship between optimism, realism and hope?
>
> What gives you hope in your daily life?
>
> Hopelessness is one of the defining features of depression, which affects one in five people at some point in their life and can end in suicide for some. It can also be an aspect of bereavement. How can we communicate a gospel of hope without trivialising such experiences?

Additional passages

Here are four passages in addition to the main one above. You could have a one-off study on a single passage, a series using all five passages, or break up a larger group into small subgroups to look at one passage each and then come back to share common themes.

> ### John 3:3–6; 16:21–22
>
> 'What is born of the Spirit is spirit'. How does this image describe the decision to be a follower of Jesus?
>
> What might the image of labour have to say about the way we tell others the good news of Jesus? How might it influence those we meet with young children, or alternatively those who are recently bereaved?
>
> What perspective do the final two verses offer on the crucifixion and resurrection of Jesus? What perspective do they offer on losing a loved one?
>
> ### Romans 5:1–5
>
> Paul describes our hope as 'sharing the glory of God'. What do you think this means?
>
> 'We also boast in our afflictions' – what does this phrase indicate about the way that we might share our experience of having Christian hope?
>
> Has there been a time in your life when endurance has relied upon hope?
>
> To what extent do you think that hope is a character trait that needs to be formed? How might hope be 'practised'?

Philippians 3:1–14

If we have 'no confidence in the flesh', what might our hope be based upon? What matters about Paul's identity here?

How does Paul relate loss to hope?

Look at verse 10–11. Do you find Paul's hesitant tone here a comfort, or does it trouble you?

Verses 12–14 describe Paul's 'pressing on'. What does this say about the value of perseverance in the light of hope?

Revelation 7:14, 17; 21:1–4

How does this picture of heaven compare with those presented by contemporary culture?

Revelation makes the move from being led as a lamb, to being led by a lamb who is a shepherd. What else is turned on its head by having a hope of what is to come?

What are the signs of heaven that you have seen on earth?

Read the last two verses. Which part of these sentences speaks most clearly to you now? Has that changed from another point in your life and faith?

Reflective sessions

These reflections use images from the natural world. Although they refer to the Bible and Christian tradition, this is in a fairly open way. These can be used with people who are sympathetic to Christianity, at least at a cultural level, but might not describe themselves as Christian.

The music, visual art and poetry are all easily available on the internet.

You might use the scripted meditation as a way into a period of silence or use it right at the end of an otherwise lively session to calm things down. It's flexible and designed to feel light touch but with the capacity to go deep.

Loving: reflective session ideas

Music

> Grayson Ives, 'A song of divine love'
>
> Maurice Duruflé, 'Ubi caritas et amor'
>
> Stormzy, 'Blinded by your grace'
>
> Samuel Wesley, 'Wash me throughly'
>
> Graham Kendrick, 'I shall be clean again'

Visual art

> Sieger Köder, *The Washing of Feet*
>
> Melani Pyke, *Potter's Hands*
>
> Michelangelo Merisi da Caravaggio, *The Taking of the Christ*
>
> Agnolo Bronzino, *The Madonna and Child with Saints*

Poetry

> Rumi, 'All through eternity'
>
> Geoffrey Anketell Studdert Kennedy, 'I know not where they have laid him'

Meditation on loving: 'Hands' by Robert Glenny

You can tell a lot about someone by how their hands look. Size or skin complexion give clues as to a person's age. Callouses or marks may point to types of employment that require working with one's hands, and tanning may indicate whether that takes place inside or outside. A wedding ring will tell you a person's marital status, as will the faded line of the place where a ring once rested. Nails, bitten or chewed might tell you that this person's hands belong to an agitated body; perfectly manicured cuticles might tell you that this person takes pleasure in the way their hands are seen and enjoyed.

And hands can also convey a vast range of human behaviours and emotions. They can be stretched out in embrace; lifted up in surrender; held gently in a moment of intimacy. Hands can point, or stroke, or wave. They can greet with the raised palm of a high-five, the powerful grasp of a handshake, or the naked aggression of a fist.

They pervade our language. Those who are a dab hand at a task may gain the upper hand on those who aren't. We lend a helping hand to those in trouble; we ask for a hand in marriage; we give a big hand to those we approve of; we avoid falling into the wrong hands. If we live hand to mouth, then we would do well not to bite the hand that feeds us. If we are unable to do anything, it may be that our hands are tied. Something imminent may be close at hand; on the other hand it may be far away.

Isaiah 49:16 talks of God's hands: God says to Israel: 'See, I have inscribed you on the palms of my hands'. Earlier in the chapter, we read 'the Lord called me before I was born' (v. 1). You were known, before you were capable of knowledge. There was no time when God's love for you was not etched into his very being. God knows you like the back of his hand.

These are hands of boundless creativity, epic scale, vast beauty and unimaginable breadth. As Graham Kendrick wrote, they are 'hands that flung stars into space'. Yet upon this everlasting canvas we find our name inscribed, and we see that tiny as we are, we are known intimately, completely and eternally. There is no time when God has known us and not loved us, or loved us and not known us.

A few days before he died, Jesus gathered with his disciples. He knows that the hour for his own departure from this world is near. He also knows that shortly he will be betrayed by Judas into the hands of the authorities, by Peter who will refuse to be recognised as his companion and by the rest who will scatter and flee. As the burden of this knowledge weighs heavy upon Jesus, still in this moment he loves them and loves them to the end. In this moment of extreme turmoil, knowledge and love meet in the most intimate of encounters. Jesus washes the feet of every disciple, removes his outer garments, emptying himself in the form of a servant to leave a legacy of love. Judas departs from their presence and Jesus tells those who remain that this is how they are to be known to others: as those who love, just as they have been loved.

When we come close to our own death we want to tell those close to us that we know them and that we love them, and we want to hear that we have been known and loved. When life ends, knowledge and love are brought together in us as they always have been in God. We can say that to our beloved with a gentle squeeze of our hands. Then we place our hands in God's and know that love makes us inseparable from them.

Letting go: reflective session ideas

Music

> Jeremy Rankin, 'God be with you till we meet again'
>
> J.S. Bach, 'Ich habe genug (BWV 82) (Simeon gladly takes leave of life having seen Christ)', first movement
>
> Peter Maxwell Davis, 'Farewell to Stromness'
>
> Jay Ungar, 'Ashokan farewell'
>
> The Beatles, 'Hello, goodbye '

Visual art

> He Qi, *Calling Disciples*
>
> J.M.W. Turner, *The Fighting Temeraire*

Poetry

> Gerald Stern, 'Waving goodbye'
>
> Dorothea Tanning, 'Woman waving to trees'
>
> Alun Lewis, 'Goodbye'
>
> T.S. Eliot, 'East Coker' from *Four Quartets*
>
> Henry Van Dyke (sometimes attributed to Victor Hugo), 'I am standing upon the seashore'

Meditation on letting go: 'Waving' by Joanna Collicutt

Waving is one of the first gestures that babies learn, and the first game we play with them is peekaboo. Both are ways of helping them to say goodbye, to let go or sit a bit more lightly to the absence of someone or something to which they are attached. When my grandchildren have to leave a playground, some human or animal friends, or to tidy away their beloved toys before bed, I am in the habit of saying 'Goodbye, train, goodbye ducks; see you another day.', a phrase I used with my own children. I suppose I want to help them to let go of these things secure in the fact that they are not lost to them forever.

Waving communicates both dignity and confidence – confidence in a universe where loved ones eventually return and confidence in our ability to inhabit the aching grief that may go with their loss. When we can no longer hear and only barely see the departing person, a distant wave on their part reassures us that they still exist, still have us in mind; and even after we have lost sight of them, we may keep on waving. Waving is a way of shrinking distance, of bridging a gap, of asserting 'I am here!'

We wave goodbye to other people; ultimately we will have to wave goodbye to our own life on this earth. But the whole of life can be thought of as a series of 'hellos' and 'goodbyes'. We wave goodbye to youthful bodies and reluctantly welcome added pounds and wrinkles; goodbye to cherished dreams that are just not going to materialise; to adorable babies as they become gangly and truculent adolescents; to an old job and familiar colleagues as we set out on a new exciting venture; to habits and conventions that have had their day; to identity-giving roles and responsibilities as retirement looms; to the family home as we move somewhere more suitable to our changing needs.

All of these goodbyes offer us the opportunity to review our priorities and, in the light of eternity, to ask ourselves, 'Are they really so important after all?' They invite us to remember that 'you can't take it with you', much as you would like to; and, as Job puts it:

> *Naked I came from my mother's womb, and naked shall I return there; the Lord gave, and the Lord has taken away; blessed be the name of the Lord.*
> JOB 1:21

Letting go is part of the life of faith. It's central to Jesus' teaching when he insists that anyone who wants to follow him needs to let go of all that is getting in the way; to sit light to money, status, popularity, even to the point of letting go of life itself. These things are not inherently bad; it is our tendency to grasp them to us that can be destructive and distracting. We need to learn to make good and gracious endings as we move through life, to say our goodbyes well, remembering that 'goodbye' is a shortened form of 'God be with you.'

In that space between two people who wave to each other stands God, always present, holding all things together. We might then perhaps think of waving as a form of blessing.

But it's also a mark of faith; of the belief that one day we will wave to say hello to more than we can ever imagine.

Seeing: reflective session ideas

Music

> Judy Garland/Eva Cassidy, 'Over the rainbow'
>
> Joni Mitchell, 'Both sides now'
>
> Claude Debussy, 'Nocturnes – clouds'
>
> Gabriel Fauré, 'Après un rêve' (After a dream)
>
> Charles Anthony Silvestri, 'Sleep'

Visual art

> Carl Larsson, *Cloud Bank over Choppy Sea*
>
> Raphael, *Sistine Madonna*

Poetry

> Thomas Traherne, 'Shadows in the water'
>
> Gerard Manley Hopkins, 'That nature is a Heraclitean fire and of the comfort of the resurrection'
>
> George Herbert, 'The elixir'
>
> R.S. Thomas, 'Wrong'

Meditation on seeing: 'Clouds' by Joanna Collicutt

There is more to life than meets the eye; things are what they seem but also more than they seem. We talk of the need to 'see through', to 'see another side', to 'see for myself'. Living in the light of heaven is an acknowledgement that there is more to life than we yet know – that there is something beyond – perhaps in the future (time) or over the horizon (space) or again behind or beneath 'the foreground of existence'.

The images of catching a glimpse through a blowing curtain, peering through a clear spot on a steamed up window, squinting through a chink in a door, 'seeing through a glass darkly', all capture this well. But perhaps above all it is clouds that convey it best – clouds in their infinite variety of colour, form and scale, beautiful and ever-changing, veiling in layer upon layer that which lies beyond, parting unbidden to reveal the wide blue yonder or pierced by rays of sunlight that promise so much. The clouds are literally heavenly:

> *The heavens are telling the glory of God, and the firmament proclaims his handiwork. Day to day pours forth speech, and night to night declares knowledge. There is no speech, nor are there words; their voice is not heard; yet their voice goes out through all the earth and their words to the end of the world.*
> PSALM 19:1–4

Our desire to see beyond the veil – for the clouds to part – is not simple curiosity about the nature of things. It is a yearning to 'see face to face', to encounter fully one who knows and loves us better than anyone else. A hospital chaplain once put it this way:

> *We say God and life and death are mysteries… not because they are unknowable, but because there is so much to know that you can never know the depths of it; there is always more you can learn… The more you learn, the more you want to know… I suppose it's faith. Belief that there is something deeply good in the mysterious heart of the infinitely knowable other.*

We will only see this clearly the other side of the grave. Yet it begins now, and if we keep our eyes open we may experience little foretastes when, as for Jesus, the clouds part and love shines through:

> *And when Jesus had been baptised, just as he came up from the water, suddenly the heavens were opened to him and he saw the God's Spirit descending like a dove and alighting on him. And a voice from the heavens said, 'This is my Son, the Beloved, with whom I am well pleased.'*
> MATTHEW 3:16–17

Growing: reflective session ideas

Music

- Samuel Barber, 'Agnus Dei'
- J.M.C. Crum, 'Now the Green Blade Riseth'
- Louis Armstrong, George Douglas, George Weiss and Bob Thiele, 'What a Wonderful World'
- Gilliam March, 'By the Mark'
- Johnny Cash and Claude Ely, 'Ain't No Grave', sung by Tom Jones

Visual art

- Vincent van Gough, *Wheat Field with Cypresses*
- Paul Serusier, *Breton dans le Champ de Ble Vert* (Breton in the green cereal field)
- Cretan fifteenth century icon, *Christ in the Tomb*

Poetry

- Raymond Foss, 'Poetry Where You Live '
- Malcolm Guite, 'Unless a Grain of Wheat'
- Gerard Manley Hopkins, 'God's Grandeur'
- Edmund Waller, 'Old Age'

Meditation on growing: 'Late blooms' by Jeremy Brooks

'Haven't you grown?' is a question that ceases to be put to us once we are past our teenage years – we are probably grateful for that. If people were particularly tactless, they may be more inclined to say 'Haven't you shrunk?' as we get older!

Yet growth is integral to living. We do not cease to grow because we cease to get taller, or wider. Our growth takes place in other ways. Our body's cells are continually being replaced. Evolutionary theory tells us that the whole of creation – the whole of the universe – is in a constant state of change and growth.

The image of the tender shoot emerging from a seed carefully planted and watered can represent so much more than simply the young whom we nurture whilst we watch them grow physically. It speaks of more than just getting bigger; but of a transformation that brings wonder and delight. How does this image apply across the whole of our lifespan, even into old age?

Each of the themes in this series of meditations represents an area of life in which we are given the opportunity to grow as we get older and as we move towards death – loving, letting go, seeing, belonging, hoping. Each of these represent gifts that are planted within us. They can be held by us tenderly and allowed to grow and blossom.

This changing and growing takes place until our dying days. William Vanstone, in his book *The Stature of Waiting* tells the extraordinary story of going to visit an elderly bishop whose life was drawing to an end. When Vanstone visits him, the bishop is confined to bed, almost blind and scarcely able to move.

> *His very posture suggested his total exposure to whatever might be done to him, his total dependence and helplessness. As one stood beside him on a particular morning some weeks before his death, one had a sudden and overwhelming impression that something of extraordinary significance was going on before one's eyes – something that even surpassed in its significance all that the bishop had done in his years of activity and achievement. ...*
>
> *He was now simply an object exposed to the world around him, receiving whatever the world might do to him; yet in his passion he seemed by no means diminished in human dignity, but rather, if that were possible, enlarged.* [12]

Growth continues to take place in us even to the very end. The truth of the gospel is that it is in, through and beyond death that we grow and become the people that we were ultimately created to be.

Belonging: reflective session ideas

Music

> Neil Diamond, 'The power of two'
>
> Benjamin Britten, 'For the flowers are great blessings (Rejoice in the Lamb)'
>
> Edward Elgar, 'Proficiscere, anima Christiana (Go forth on thy journey, Christian soul) (The dream of Gerontius)'
>
> Frederick Delius, 'The walk to the paradise garden (A village Romeo and Juliet)'
>
> Johannes Brahms, 'How lovely is your dwelling place'

Visual art

> Stanley Spencer, *Christ in the Wilderness – Consider the Lilies*
>
> Vincent van Gogh, *Sunflowers 4*
>
> John Ruskin, *Study of Quatrefoil Fringed Gentian*

Poetry

> Mary Oliver, 'Daisies'
>
> Mary Oliver, 'When death comes'
>
> Robert Herrick, 'To daffodils'

Meditation on belonging: 'Meadow flowers' by Joanna Collicutt

We are all different. It's not simply that there are different species, or tribes, or families; each individual is unique and particular. We probably don't stop and think about this enough.

The Victorian writer John Ruskin said: 'An animal must be either one animal or another animal: it cannot be a general animal, or it is no animal.'[13]

We realise this when we attempt to replace a pet that has died with another of the same breed. The new cat or dog or whatever may be the spitting image of the one we loved and lost, but it is not that one. It is simply itself. And like its predecessor, it cannot be replaced. What's more, this is true for the little things that we might not normally notice. If you look closely at the daisies springing up among the grass in your garden or a park, it becomes clear that each flower is just a little different from its neighbours.

It's also true for us. People sometimes say in a eulogy, 'They broke the mould when they made him.' But of course there is no mould to break.

We are each unique creations. The natural order is one of almost unimaginable extravagance. Every bit of it is bespoke.

The fact that we are singular, unique and irreplaceable should remind us that each human life is a precious treasure; each of us matters – not on account of what we do or have or of where we have come from or what we have achieved – but simply because we are. This is what Jesus seems to be getting at when he invites his followers to consider the lilies and the birds; he reminds them that what may in human terms appear at first glance to be just an example of a type and thus of little worth – two a penny – is instead treasured as a significant individual by God. Not only that, Jesus remarks on the beauty of the flowers. The extravagance of creation is not simply about variety and proliferation; it is about glory.

But this sense of uniqueness can sometimes seem a burden as much as a blessing. Being the only one of anything can feel lonely. That's perhaps why we like those quizzes that tell us what type of personality we have. It means we can identify with a group. For, after all, we are social animals and we need to belong.

Yet we make a mistake if we think our uniqueness cuts us off from others. Ruskin put his finger on it when he wrote:

> *In differing [from his fellow], each assumes a relation to, his fellow; they are no more each the repetition of the other, they are parts of a system; and each implies and is connected with the existence of the rest.*[14]

Just as each individual daisy forms part of a clump or carpet of flowers and has its own place both there and in the meadow in which it grows, so we each have our place in the diverse body that is the human race, and beyond it in the cosmos. We are singular but part of a system. We are small yet we are part of something bigger. We have our special place, and we have our allotted time.

And when our time comes and we face our singular death alone, we find that, in the words of the writer to the Hebrews:

> *You have come to… the heavenly Jerusalem, and to innumerable angels in festal gathering, and to the assembly of the firstborn who are enrolled in heaven, and to God the judge of all, and to the spirits of the righteous made perfect, and to Jesus.*
> HEBREWS 12:22–24

Hoping: reflective session ideas

Music

> Anton Bruckner: 'Ave Maria'
>
> Robert Bridges: 'All my hope on God is founded' (Herbert Howells wrote the now synonymous tune 'Michael' after finding these words following the death of his son)
>
> Johannes Brahms: 'Lord, let me know my end'
>
> U2: 'I still haven't found what I'm looking for'
>
> J.S. Bach, 'St Matthew Passion' (BWV 244), final movement: 'We sit down in tears'

Visual art

> Henry Alexander Bowler, *The Doubt – Can These Dry Bones Live?*
>
> Sieger Koder, *Maternal Womb*
>
> Russian fifteenth century icon, *Deposition in the Tomb*

Poetry

> Author unknown, 'I believe in the sun even when it isn't shining. I believe in love even when I am alone. I believe in God even when he is silent.'
>
> Horatio Spafford, 'It is well with my soul' – read the story behind this famous hymn:
> en.wikipedia.org/wiki/It_Is_Well_with_My_Soul

Meditation on hoping: 'Birth' by Robert Glenny

The experiences of the beginning and the end of life are more closely connected than perhaps we first realise.

Both are moments finely poised between taking control and letting go; both involve toil, endurance and pain, and both offer a perspective on hope. Dying is something that we do alone, and which no one else can do on our behalf or experience for us. It's when we let go, finally, of our earthly bodies. Labour is the act of becoming alone again, the first time in months that a body is not cohabiting with another life. It is simultaneously a moment of creation and a moment of loss.

The developing independence of children who grow up is also the most profound type of loss. J.K. Rowling captures it beautifully in her novel *The Casual Vacancy* as a mother reflects on her now teenage boy:

> *How awful it was, thought Tessa, remembering Fats the toddler, the way tiny ghosts of your living children haunted your heart; they could never know, and would hate it if they did, how their growing was a constant bereavement.*[15]

For those who give birth, a child represents not just hope but also what was once a part of you that you can no longer control. The inescapable relationship between hope and disappointment, between gift and loss, uniquely expressed in bringing up a child, begins with labour.

There is an extraordinary and profound way in which the life of Jesus is prefigured by the labour of Mary. Like all mothers, her own body is literally broken, with blood and water flowing out, to give life to her child. It happens at the beginning of his life, as well as at its end. 'See from his head, his hands, his feet,' wrote Isaac Watts, 'Sorrow and love flow mingled down!' We don't often apply those words to Jesus' birth. Perhaps we should.

And yet for all of the effort and pain and exhaustion of labour, it is still an intensely hopeful act. After my son was born, my wife said to me that 'What helps to make sense of labour is the knowledge that it is not just painful but purposeful.' There is something intimate and wonderful on the other side; a banquet of delight beyond the vale of shadow. It's what we hold fast to during the moments of calm between the contractions of grief when we are bereaved.

The story of Jesus begins with the hope that precedes his birth and ends with the hope that follows his death. Both hopes are subverted. Jesus is born with the hopes of a nation resting upon his tiny shoulders. It turns out he's not quite the Messiah that Israel was preparing for, and ultimately that it could not receive. At his death, it seems that those hopes have been finally and brutally dashed. As the life drains away from him, Jesus finds breath to speak to his mother – there at the beginning, and there at the end. 'Woman, this is now your son', he says. These words are definitively hopeful because even in the depths of despair, Jesus reassures us that others are there to take care of us. Here Jesus begins the work of reforming his scattered community of companions by trusting them to hope. Two days later as he rises, he reforms the notion that death has the final word and so embodies a resurrection hope. At the foot of the cross, this new community and new hope is birthed.

Prayer stations

The prayer walk comprises six stations (stops) following the six themes of loving, letting go, seeing, growing, belonging and hoping. Each can be used individually, but they can be combined into a walk to and from Emmaus (Luke 24:13–35). The story represents human life, death and resurrection in a single narrative and can help the participant to rediscover what it is really important in life.

Each prayer station consists of a simple arrangement of objects, instructions for the participant and a short printed prayer to take home. The stations are designed by Julie Mintern and the photographs are by Jo Ind.

Setting up a prayer walk

> Set up the walk inside or outside, in a church, school, or other community space.
>
> Set up the stations as a journey that moves spiritually inwards to Station 3 and begins to turn spiritually outwards at Station 4. (Recall that the two on the road to Emmaus turned round and went back.) You might want to do this as a horseshoe but the precise way you do this will depend on the space you have available.
>
> Mark the route with footprints (template on p. 100–101) if you wish.
>
> Use the walk either with the sermon starters, Bible studies or meditations on the same six living well themes or just on its own.
>
> It may be particularly fitting to do this at Eastertide or at Remembrance tide. You might also want to provide copies of the prayer that participants can take away.
>
> You will need:
>
> > Prayer walk directions to be left at the start (p. 90)
> >
> > Bible passage in different versions also to be left at the start (pp. 91, 92, 93)
> >
> > For each station: 'focus, act, pray' prompts, materials, paper slips with the prayer printed on them in a basket or bowl
> >
> > Footprints cut from adhesive paper if desired (template on p. 100–101).

Prayer walk directions

You are invited to enter into
your Emmaus Road prayer journey.

This is a special journey designed to help us think about how
death and loss tell us what is really important in life.

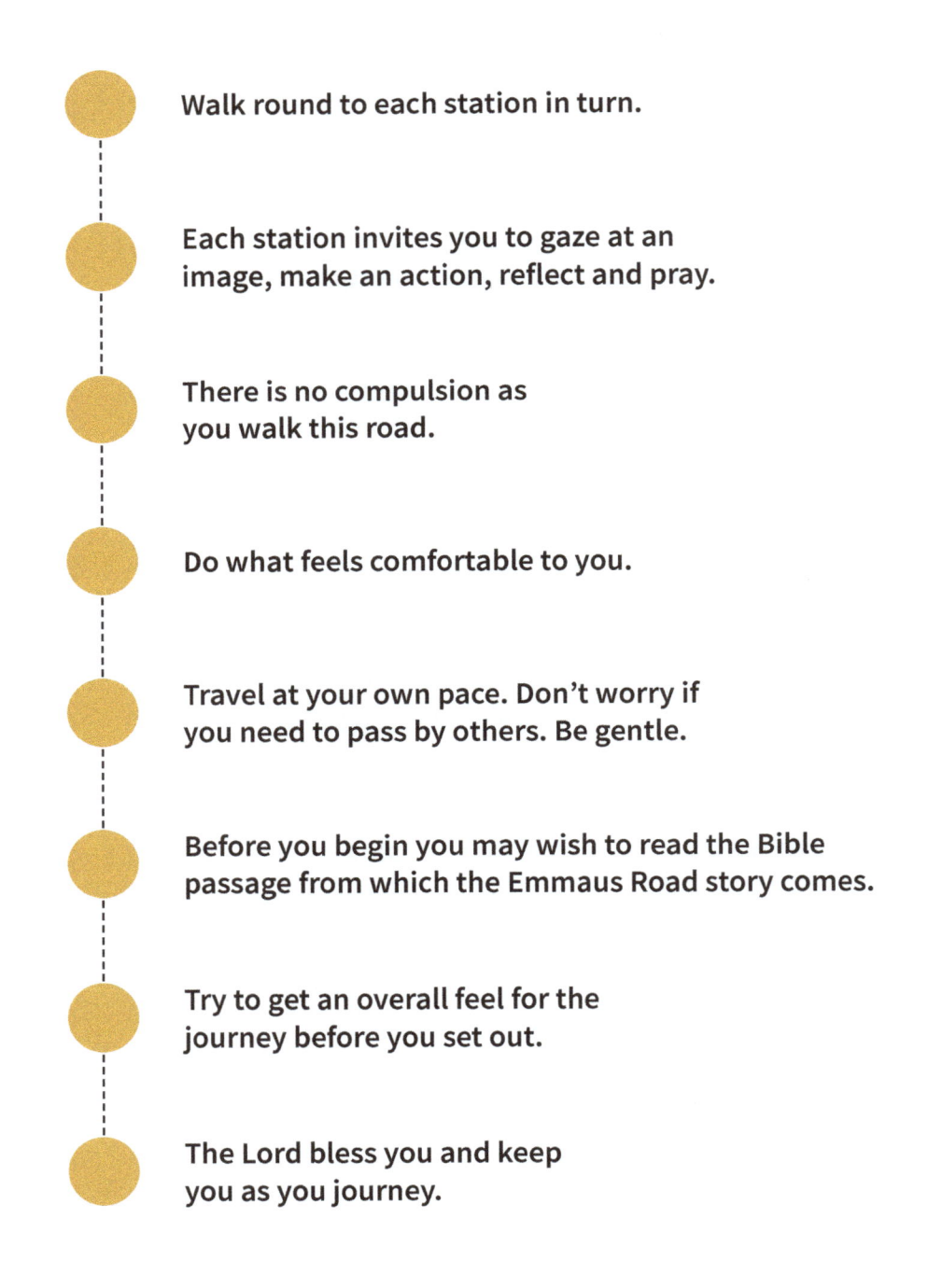

- Walk round to each station in turn.

- Each station invites you to gaze at an image, make an action, reflect and pray.

- There is no compulsion as you walk this road.

- Do what feels comfortable to you.

- Travel at your own pace. Don't worry if you need to pass by others. Be gentle.

- Before you begin you may wish to read the Bible passage from which the Emmaus Road story comes.

- Try to get an overall feel for the journey before you set out.

- The Lord bless you and keep you as you journey.

Luke 24:13–36 (NRSV)

The Road to Emmaus

Now on that same day two of them were going to a village called Emmaus, about seven miles from Jerusalem, and talking with each other about all these things that had happened. While they were talking and discussing, Jesus himself came near and went with them, but their eyes were kept from recognising him. And he said to them, 'What are you discussing with each other while you walk along?' They stood still, looking sad. Then one of them, whose name was Cleopas, answered him, 'Are you the only stranger in Jerusalem who does not know the things that have taken place there in these days?' He asked them, 'What things?'

They replied, 'The things about Jesus of Nazareth, who was a prophet mighty in deed and word before God and all the people, and how our chief priests and leaders handed him over to be condemned to death and crucified him. But we had hoped that he was the one to redeem Israel. Yes, and besides all this, it is now the third day since these things took place. Moreover, some women of our group astounded us. They were at the tomb early this morning, and when they did not find his body there, they came back and told us that they had indeed seen a vision of angels who said that he was alive. Some of those who were with us went to the tomb and found it just as the women had said; but they did not see him.' Then he said to them, 'Oh, how foolish you are, and how slow of heart to believe all that the prophets have declared! Was it not necessary that the Messiah should suffer these things and then enter into his glory?' Then beginning with Moses and all the prophets, he interpreted to them the things about himself in all the scriptures.

As they came near the village to which they were going, he walked ahead as if he were going on. But they urged him strongly, saying, 'Stay with us, because it is almost evening and the day is now nearly over.' So he went in to stay with them. When he was at the table with them, he took bread, blessed and broke it, and gave it to them. Then their eyes were opened, and they recognised him; and he vanished from their sight. They said to each other, 'Were not our hearts burning within us while he was talking to us on the road, while he was opening the scriptures to us?' That same hour they got up and returned to Jerusalem; and they found the eleven and their companions gathered together. They were saying, 'The Lord has risen indeed, and he has appeared to Simon!' Then they told what had happened on the road, and how he had been made known to them in the breaking of the bread. While they were talking about this, Jesus himself stood among them and said to them, 'Peace be with you.'

Luke 24:13–36 (NIV)

The Road to Emmaus

Now that same day two of them were going to a village called Emmaus, about seven miles from Jerusalem. They were talking with each other about everything that had happened. As they talked and discussed these things with each other, Jesus himself came up and walked along with them; but they were kept from recognising him. He asked them, 'What are you discussing together as you walk along?' They stood still, their faces downcast. One of them, named Cleopas, asked him, 'Are you the only one visiting Jerusalem who does not know the things that have happened there in these days?' 'What things?' he asked.

'About Jesus of Nazareth,' they replied. 'He was a prophet, powerful in word and deed before God and all the people. The chief priests and our rulers handed him over to be sentenced to death, and they crucified him; but we had hoped that he was the one who was going to redeem Israel. And what is more, it is the third day since all this took place. In addition, some of our women amazed us. They went to the tomb early this morning but didn't find his body. They came and told us that they had seen a vision of angels, who said he was alive. Then some of our companions went to the tomb and found it just as the women had said, but they did not see Jesus.' He said to them, 'How foolish you are, and how slow to believe all that the prophets have spoken! Did not the Messiah have to suffer these things and then enter his glory?' And beginning with Moses and all the Prophets, he explained to them what was said in all the Scriptures concerning himself.

As they approached the village to which they were going, Jesus continued on as if he were going farther. But they urged him strongly, 'Stay with us, for it is nearly evening; the day is almost over.' So he went in to stay with them. When he was at the table with them, he took bread, gave thanks, broke it and began to give it to them. Then their eyes were opened and they recognised him, and he disappeared from their sight. They asked each other, 'Were not our hearts burning within us while he talked with us on the road and opened the Scriptures to us?'

They got up and returned at once to Jerusalem. There they found the Eleven and those with them, assembled together and saying, 'It is true! The Lord has risen and has appeared to Simon.' Then the two told what had happened on the way, and how Jesus was recognised by them when he broke the bread. While they were still talking about this, Jesus himself stood among them and said to them, 'Peace be with you.'

Luke 24:13–36 (MSG)

The Road to Emmaus

That same day two of them were walking to the village Emmaus, about seven miles out of Jerusalem. They were deep in conversation, going over all these things that had happened. In the middle of their talk and questions, Jesus came up and walked along with them. But they were not able to recognise who he was. He asked, 'What's this you're discussing so intently as you walk along?' They just stood there, long-faced, like they had lost their best friend. Then one of them, his name was Cleopas, said, 'Are you the only one in Jerusalem who hasn't heard what's happened during the last few days?' He said, 'What has happened?'

They said, 'The things that happened to Jesus the Nazarene. He was a man of God, a prophet, dynamic in work and word, blessed by both God and all the people. Then our high priests and leaders betrayed him, got him sentenced to death, and crucified him. And we had our hopes up that he was the One, the One about to deliver Israel. And it is now the third day since it happened. But now some of our women have completely confused us. Early this morning they were at the tomb and couldn't find his body. They came back with the story that they had seen a vision of angels who said he was alive. Some of our friends went off to the tomb to check and found it empty just as the women said, but they didn't see Jesus.' Then he said to them, 'So thick-headed! So slow-hearted! Why can't you simply believe all that the prophets said? Don't you see that these things had to happen, that the Messiah had to suffer and only then enter into his glory?' Then he started at the beginning, with the Books of Moses, and went on through all the Prophets, pointing out everything in the Scriptures that referred to him.

They came to the edge of the village where they were headed. He acted as if he were going on but they pressed him: 'Stay and have supper with us. It's nearly evening; the day is done.' So he went in with them. And here is what happened: He sat down at the table with them. Taking the bread, he blessed and broke and gave it to them. At that moment, open-eyed, wide-eyed, they recognised him. And then he disappeared. Back and forth they talked. 'Didn't we feel on fire as he conversed with us on the road, as he opened up the Scriptures for us?' They didn't waste a minute. They were up and on their way back to Jerusalem. They found the Eleven and their friends gathered together, talking away: 'It's really happened! The Master has been raised up – Simon saw him!' Then the two went over everything that happened on the road and how they recognised him when he broke the bread. While they were saying all this, Jesus appeared to them and said, 'Peace be with you.'

Loving: prayer station

Focus

Jesus himself came near to them… they stood still looking sad.
LUKE 24:15–16

Action

Pick up a holding cross and move your hand over the rosemary. Smell the living rosemary, recall your loss and gaze upon Jesus. Take time, ask Jesus to come near, to listen, to understand and guide you.

Pray

Lord, grief is the price we pay for love. Help me to trust that in my sadness you draw near. Amen.

(Materials: holding crosses; sprigs of fresh rosemary; slips printed with 'Lord, grief is the price we pay for love. Help me to trust that in my sadness you draw near. Amen.')

Letting go: prayer station

Focus

'But we had hoped that he was the one to redeem Israel… Stay with us, because it is almost evening and the day is now nearly over.'
LUKE 24:21, 29

Action

Think about a loss, a disappointment or an unfulfilled dream. Use a pen and write your loss on a stone. Place it in the basket.

Pray

Lord, be with me as I mourn my 'might have beens'. Help me to leave them in your hands. Amen.

(Materials: a small basket of flat pebbles; two or three Sharpie pens; slips printed with 'Lord, be with me as I mourn my "might have beens". Help me to leave them in your hands. Amen.')

Seeing: prayer station

Focus

When he was at the table with them, he took bread, blessed and broke it, and gave it to them. Then their eyes were opened.
LUKE 24:30–31

Action

Tear off a piece of bread. Break it and look carefully at it as you pray and then eat it.

Pray

Lord, you are the one who feeds me. Open my eyes and help me to see more than meets the eye. Amen.

(Materials: a plate with a small piece of fresh bread; a gluten-free alternative; slips printed with 'Lord, you are the one who feeds me. Open my eyes and help me to see more than meets the eye. Amen.')

Growing: prayer station

Focus

'Were not our hearts burning within us while he was talking to us on the road?'... That same hour they got up... Then they told what had happened.
LUKE 24:32–35

Action

Light a candle and look in the mirror. See yourself as God sees you at this moment, full of potential.

Pray

Lord, thank you that I am precious and loved by you. Help me to grow through the dark times as I journey on. Strengthen me to own and tell my story, safe in the knowledge you have called me by name – I am yours. Amen.

(Materials: a medium-sized mirror that can be propped up safely; a supply of tea lights or small candles; means of lighting the candles; slips printed with 'Lord, thank you that I am precious and loved by you. Help me to grow through the dark times as I journey on. Strengthen me to own and tell my story, safe in the knowledge you have called me by name – I am yours. Amen.')

Belonging: prayer station

Focus

They returned to Jerusalem; and they found the eleven and their companions gathered together.
LUKE 24:33

Action

Write your name along with any other names you want to remember on a bird(s) and add them to the prayer tree. We become ourselves in the company of others.

Pray

Lord, thank you for all who have loved me and those I have loved. Bring us all to that place where there is no more sorrow or sighing, where the joys and pains of humanity are held in your eternal arms of love and peace. Amen.

(Materials: a 'prayer tree' either bought or homemade from twigs or branches, or an appropriate shrub in a pot; a supply of pens; birds on strong paper or light card (template on p. 102), pieces of ribbon or string to attach to 'tree'; slips printed with 'Lord, thank you for all who have loved me and those I have loved. Bring us all to that place where there is no more sorrow or sighing, where the joys and pains of humanity are held in your eternal arms of love and peace. Amen.')

Hoping: prayer station

Focus

Jesus stood among them and said to them 'Peace be with you.'
LUKE 24:36

Action

Smell the flower and, as you do so, enjoy the peace and memories of your loved ones. Run your fingers through the lavender plant. Let it calm you. Offer your cares to God and ask him to give you his peace.

Pray

Lord, help me to trust that death is not the end. Keep me fixed on the hope that we will one day meet face to face and give me the peace that passes all understanding. Amen.

(Materials: fragrant flowers in a small vase; sprigs of fresh lavender; slips printed with 'Lord, help me to trust that death is not the end. Keep me fixed on the hope that we will one day meet face to face and give me the peace that passes all understanding. Amen.')

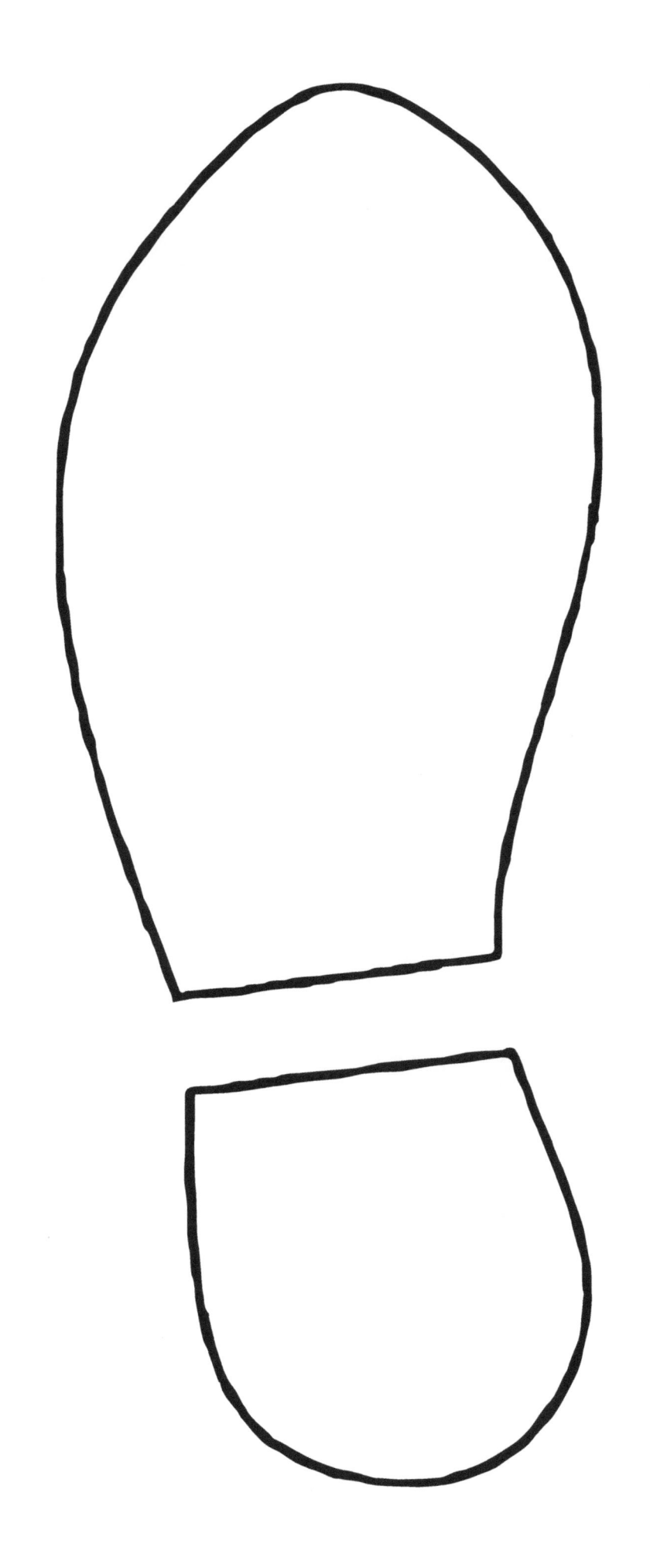

Living well in the light of mortality 101

102 DEATH AND LIFE

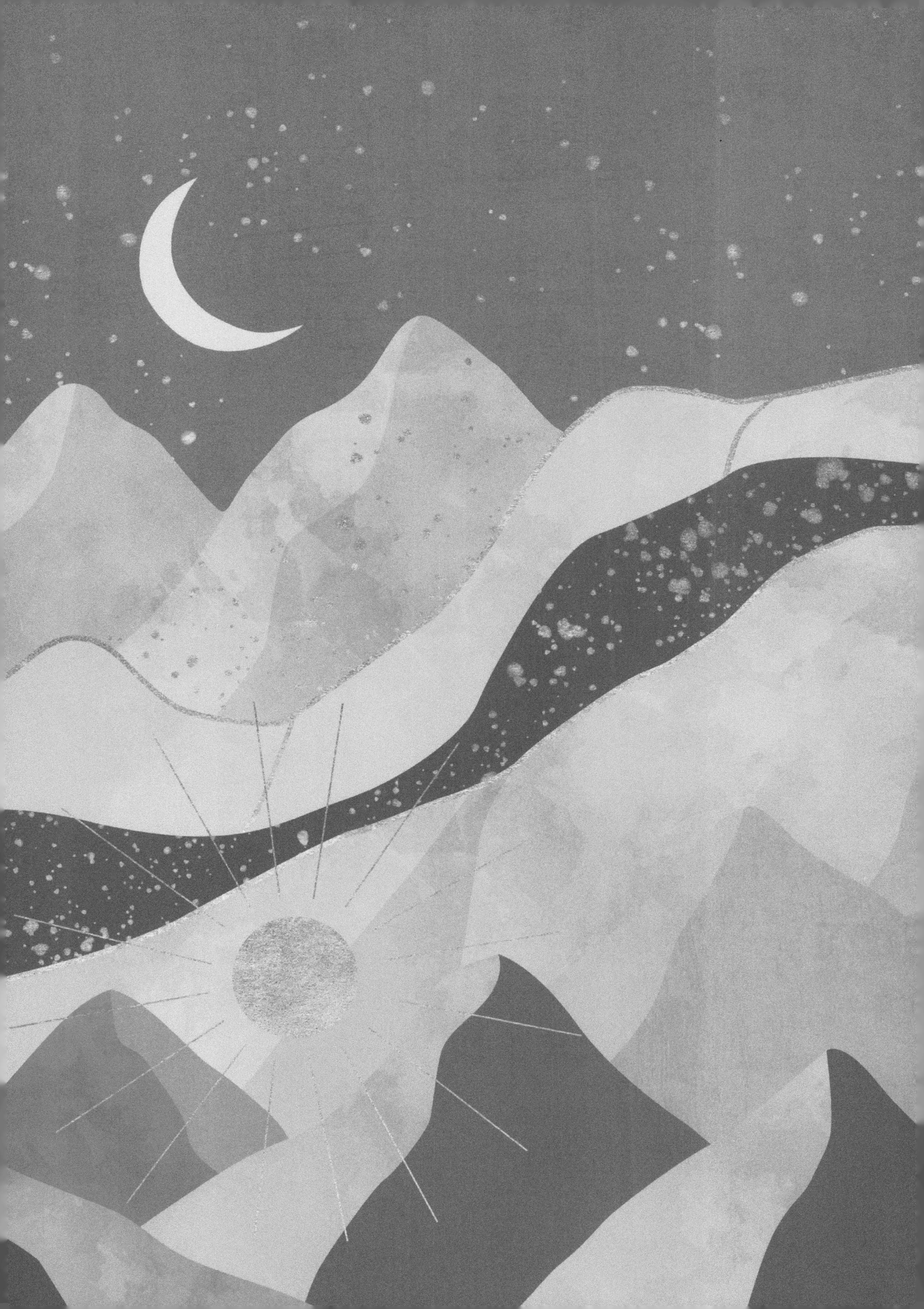

Preparing for death

Running a Well-Prepared course

The following pages contain material to help you plan and deliver a course enabling people – old or young, fit or frail – to prepare well for their last months on this earth. Supporting people in preparing for the momentous physical, emotional and spiritual challenge posed by dying is a high calling but is also a demanding one. So, before you begin it is good to pause and to ask some prayerful questions.

Why?

Why do I/we want to do this?

> Perhaps you've been inspired by attending a talk or workshop on preparing for death and dying.
>
> Perhaps you've been feeling frustrated that your pastoral ministry isn't quite getting to the heart of things or that it's getting stale.
>
> Perhaps you see this as a way of drawing more people into your church or, conversely, of reaching out in service to the wider community.
>
> Perhaps someone has simply asked you to do this.

Each of us will have our own answer to this question.

Reflecting critically on your motives will help you gauge your degree of commitment to this particular form of ministry or whether something less demanding of time, energy and emotion would do the job. If you decide to go ahead it will help you in designing and publicising the course. It will also help you evaluate its 'success'. For example, you may find that the course didn't attract any new people to your church but that you got to know and value some of your existing congregation in a new and deeper way, or made new contacts in your local community. The course would have been unsuccessful in one respect but successful in another, and your evaluation of its overall success would depend on your motives at the start.

A second rather different question is: 'Why should any church consider doing this?', to which there is an answer that applies to us all. The certainty of the resurrection is what gives Christians our identity, and the message we proclaim and try to live out is of life in the midst of death and hope in the midst of loss. We have something significant to say on this matter. What's more, the resurrection is our 'USP'. None of the secular groups that specialise in preparing people for death, good as many of them are, can offer hope of eternal life.

Of course, we will each have our own personal take on what the words 'resurrection' and 'eternal life' mean for us. Most people who have run Well-Prepared courses say they develop a deeper sense of this through honest conversations with others that involve wondering, reflecting, explaining, telling stories and listening.

Talking with folk about our common mortality, being alongside them in the 'valley of the shadow of death' and offering a message of Christian hope is part of the calling of all Christians – it's not an optional extra. Clergy from many denominations make a specific promise at ordination to 'prepare the dying for their death.' This has traditionally been interpreted as deathbed ministry, but we are all dying from the day we are born and we do not know when our hour will come, so it's never too early to prepare.

Perhaps the clearest finding of our research is that older people in particular are very keen – 'desperate' is not too strong a word – to talk about death and dying, both the practicalities and the spiritual aspects. Yet they all too often find that others are reluctant to have these sorts of conversations, and it's ironic that most churches don't offer this opportunity either.

Running a formal structured course is only one of several ways of doing this, and after reading the next few sections you may decide that it isn't for you at this time. But if you do go ahead with your eyes open, our research suggests that this will be one of the most rewarding things you have done in ministry. Some of the potential benefits include:

> Achieving a deep sense of intimacy with course participants;
>
> Regaining a sense of what Christian ministry and service is all about;
>
> Having the experience of meeting a pressing human spiritual need;
>
> Developing your pastoral skills;
>
> Broadening your knowledge-base in this area;
>
> Gaining confidence in talking about big theological questions;
>
> Being held and supported by a structure that others have tried and tested;
>
> Learning to appreciate the life-wisdom and spiritual insights of course participants;
>
> Allowing yourself to receive care from others (course participants and co-facilitator);
>
> Growing spiritually through articulating and owning your own authentic perspective on these issues and seeing where more work might need to be done.

When?

When should you do it?

Timing is not a trivial consideration. The New Testament makes a lot of the timing of the passion and death of Jesus (Matthew 26:18) and of the timing of his eventual return (1 Corinthians 4:5). In a similar way much of our conception of death relates to time – 'my time is running out', 'her time had come', 'his death was untimely' and so on. There is a sense in which God's time and our time come together at the moment of death. So, in deciding to prepare for this moment we are recognising that all our plans are provisional and that our time on earth is limited; we catch a glimpse of an eternal perspective.

Running a Well-Prepared course also takes time. The material in this handbook is for a series of six 90-minute weekly meetings. On top of this there is planning time, and the course facilitators need to build in additional time for emotional 'decompression'. One of us provided homemade cake for her course and found that the time spent baking the cakes became quite special, allowing her to become calm and to focus, and to step into a mindset of prayerful tender care – but it added to the preparation time. (Of course it's not essential to provide homemade cakes, but our research indicates that providing a hospitable setting over which care has evidently been taken is one of the key ingredients to a successful course.) So, choose a period which is less busy than others and, if necessary, drop some of your usual commitments for a while.

You will also need to consider personal aspects of your timing. It's usually not wise to do this sort of work if you are recently bereaved. On the other hand, at certain periods in our lives we may be losing older relatives and friends on a fairly regular basis, so finding a bereavement-free slot may not be entirely realistic. A lot depends on how emotionally resilient you are at the time, and it is a good idea to discuss your particular situation with those who know you well.

These principles also apply to potential course participants; certain individuals may not be in the best frame of mind to benefit from the course at a particular time, but, unlike the facilitators, they can always decide to pull out if it becomes too challenging. More widely there can be seasons in the life of a community where this seems to be just the right thing to do, and other times when it clearly is not.

The time of day and year when you hold the course will depend on the needs of your participants. In general, older people do not like to venture out on winter evenings. It has been traditional to talk about death around Remembrance Sunday and All Souls' Day, but this coincides with the evenings starting to draw in. Instead, it may be easier for people of all ages to approach this potentially dark and gloomy subject at a time when the days are lengthening (during Lent or after Easter) or in early autumn when nature's preparation for sleep appears so beautiful. Beauty not only gives us pleasure; it can communicate meaning and instil peace.

Where?

Where should you hold it?

The key aspects of your chosen environment are that it should feel safe and hospitable.

There are pros and cons to running a course in a church. The pros are that churches are often beautiful spaces that encourage reflection; older churches will be full of reminders both that we die but also that we can leave a legacy of memories behind us; access to a pleasant churchyard can be even more helpful[16] and, if the weather permits, you might hold one or more sessions outside. On the other hand, churches can feel creepy and can be places of bad memories for some; it may be difficult for people to connect what is said in this special environment with their ordinary daily lives; churches are not always physically accessible or comfortable.

Running a course in someone's home has the advantage of providing a feeling of hospitable domesticity, but it is probably not a good idea. The space is too personal for someone to get up and leave without appearing rude. It can be difficult to voice disagreement with someone if you are in their home. The room in which feelings of grief or fear have been expressed may become a difficult place for the host to feel relaxed after the participants have departed.

So, ideally the course should be held in a more neutral space such as a church room or a community facility, which has good access and, ideally, with a loop system in place. You will need facilities for making a hot drink, and toilets. It's important that participants can see out and feel they can get out easily. A café style arrangement works well, but it may on occasion be good to arrange chairs in a horseshoe facing a window (especially if the view is pleasant and restful or busy and full of 'normal' life). This dilutes the intensity of the experience, gives a broader perspective, and allows participants to 'zone out' as necessary and spend time with their own thoughts.

A further option is to run a bespoke group in a residential home or sheltered housing setting. Again, choosing a safe, hospitable, private and neutral space within this setting will be an important part of your planning.

Who?

Who are the intended participants?

You will need to decide whether the course is run as part of the programme of an existing group whose members already know each other (for example a Mothers' Union, a carers' support group, or residents in a care home) or whether it is a stand-alone event. You may want to offer it for all ages of adult or target a specific age group. You may want to run an ecumenical group or to open it to people in your locality of all faiths and none. Your decision on this will affect the content of your sessions (though perhaps not as much as you might think). It will also affect the way you contact potential participants. It's wise to have an upper limit on group size; 12–15 participants is a reasonable maximum.

These courses are communities of mutual learning in which the facilitators may gain as much as the participants. One course facilitator who kept a journal to record her experiences said: 'I'm on the same journey… it's not just me leading a group of others but the same issues that I am inviting them to engage with I engage with myself.'

Who will run the course?

You will need help and support in running a course; there should be at least two facilitators for each session. If there are two facilitators one person can be giving the main input while the other is on hand to deal with practical issues or to attend to anyone who becomes distressed or is in danger of dominating discussions. This is all part of sensitive handling of group dynamics, so that one person doesn't take over the whole session and impose their agenda on it, and the more reticent members of the group can be drawn out.

The facilitators can support each other and offer constructive feedback. Recall that Jesus sent out disciples in pairs (Luke 10:1). Our research also indicates that there should be continuity, so at least one of the facilitators should be there throughout the course even if you invite guest speakers for certain sessions.

The facilitators do not need to have all the practical and theological answers about death and dying. Instead you need to be prepared by having reflected honestly and prayerfully about your attitude to and experience of this area. (There are some exercises on pages 136–41 to help you do this.) You also need to have some experience of being alongside people who are questioning, confused, or in distress, to be prepared to listen openly to them, to tolerate uncertainty and to be okay with acknowledging mystery and admitting that you don't know.

But you also need to have a clear sense of the basis of your hope so that you can communicate this feeling to others with a sense of authenticity. You may not have all the 'head' answers but you do need to have heartfelt assurance. This will not be based so much on the sort of theology to be found in the creeds or academic textbooks but more on your lived experience of God, and it might be felt as inner convictions rather like these:

> God is love and wants to give us our hearts' desires;
>
> God is with us and will never let us go;
>
> God is just – not capricious or cruel – and knows each person's back story;

> The facts are friendly (because in Jesus, God acted decisively to redeem this broken world);
>
> The human body is precious and important (because Jesus' body was precious and important – even after death).

Convictions like these don't necessarily have to be spelt out to others (though you may find yourself expressing them on occasion). It's more that these will be the foundation on which everything you say and do rests, and they will be picked up intuitively by the participants.

How?

Death is frightening, in both its physical and existential aspects.

It was Sigmund Freud who first pointed out that we deal with frightening stuff by pushing it right to the back of our minds. We do this both as individuals and as a society. In 21st-century Britain, the process of caring for the dying and managing death has been largely handed over to professionals. This means that we can avoid engaging with it until a close loved one dies, and for many of us this does not happen until middle age. Indeed it is possible for us to go through our whole life without ever having seen the body of a person who has died.

So, inviting people to talk about death is inviting them to do something that may well break the habits of a lifetime; it will involve stepping into unknown and possibly scary territory.

This means that the facilitators need to lead the participants into this place with a mix of gentleness and confidence, a step at a time. Psalm 23 talks of the comfort provided by the Lord's rod and staff as the psalmist walks through the valley of the shadow of death. This comfort can be provided by two things – the way the course is structured and the provision of a 'holding environment' by the facilitators. Ways of doing this are explored in the next two sections.

How to structure the course

Imagine that you are exploring the ocean with some novice divers. The movement is down and away from the light, noise and fresh air of everyday life into a place that is dark and disorienting but full of treasures, followed by a gradual return to normality. You need a good oxygen supply yourself (hence the need for personal preparation), and you need to be able to signal clearly to your pupils to indicate where they are, what is happening and whether or not things are okay. Each session may take them a little deeper, but they always return to the light. Running a Well-Prepared course is very like this.

Each session of the course should have the same structure, almost like a ritual. You will need to signal the beginning and the end clearly. One way of signalling the end of the session is to say the same prayer every time; this reminds the participants that we are all in God's hands and is a calming way to give closure. If your group consists of people from different faith backgrounds a good prayer to use is based on Number 6:24–26:

The Lord [or God] bless you and keep you; the Lord [or God] make his face to shine upon you and be gracious to you; the Lord [or God] lift up his countenance upon you and give you peace.

As already noted, it is important to offer time and space for decompression – a kind of buffer zone between the emotionally significant material and mundane life. Half an hour for sharing tea and cake after an hour's session is ideal.

Just as each session can be thought of as a journey into the deep and back again, so can the whole course. This is why the most emotionally challenging material (the physical reality of death) is best dealt with in the middle of the course, led into gradually via practical sessions and followed by more emotionally comforting content. You should give some attention to the way that you end the whole course and the process of parting.

The whole journey must feel as safe as possible. This can be helped a lot by providing good information – a flyer (for a template see page 142) setting out clearly what participants can expect and a verbal summary at the beginning of each session; people shouldn't be taken by surprise. It is also important to set some confidentiality boundaries such as 'Chatham House rules'; people need to know that what they have shared remains within the group.[17]

You should give some thought to follow-up. If participants have continuing needs or questions that have been opened up by attending the course, is there someone you can point them to after it has finished so that they are not left unsupported? In the case where you are pastorally responsible for some or all of the participants, follow-up may involve a personal visit, encouraging participants to continue to meet on their own, recommending some further reading, or it may mean planning another event in your church such as a service of remembrance, a quiet day, or a series of sermons. Be realistic about what you can offer within the resources available to you.

How to provide a 'holding environment'

When working pastorally with people who are engaging with the prospect of their own death you will need to give out signals that they will be 'held' as they experience and struggle with distressing feelings. You will not rub their noses in these feelings, but will instead support them in regulating themselves as they establish their own balance between raw emotion and coping strategies such as humour and practical chat. You will need to go with their flow.

If someone wants to leave the group for a few minutes, or to go home, or to miss a session because the topic seems too challenging, that is fine; they are simply taking responsibility for managing their own emotions. If someone becomes quietly distressed in a group session but does not choose to leave that is fine also; here you need to keep the tone relaxed and unfussy, showing that it is okay – in fact, normal – to express emotion in these circumstances.

Having a box of tissues to hand is always useful, but remember that tears are not the only way that people express distress; be attentive to people's facial expressions and body language.

It's worth being aware of two natural healing processes that can be harnessed as part of providing a holding environment. The first is called 'reciprocal inhibition'. This is where two activities work against each other: we cannot eat or play when we are afraid and, conversely, nice food and a playful ambience both reduce fear. As someone once put it, 'If you're eating cake you know you're not dead.' Our research findings showed that course participants really appreciated humour and laughter, which, much to their surprise, transformed an experience that could have been very gloomy into fun.

The second healing process is called 'habituation'. This is grounded in our biology. It describes the almost universal experience that when we confront the thing that we have been avoiding it can be very unpleasant at first, but our initial discomfort will decrease to manageable levels fairly quickly. If we stick with it we will go on to experience a sense of mastery and achievement, so that the next encounter is much less difficult and our confidence builds. Trusting this process of habituation to do its work by keeping a calm demeanour and communicating a sense that all will be well is part of what it means to provide a holding environment.

How to support participants in their learning

The need to be pastorally sensitive should not mislead you into thinking of the sessions as 'therapy'. This is a course in which participants will be reflecting and learning, not a therapy programme. So, providing a holding environment is not an end in itself but a starting point for learning.

Different people have different preferred learning styles. They also have different learning histories. Some will have really enjoyed school; others may associate school with bullying, humiliation and failure. Some respond well to group discussion; others want to be talked at. Some love music and the visual arts; they leave others cold. Some like the internet; others (especially older people or those on low incomes) find it difficult to access. Some want to plumb emotional and spiritual depths; others want to dip their toe in the water. When trying to facilitate exploration of death and dying it pays to have several flexible modes of delivery to suit the individual(s) and the situation.

In our research we found that the favourite sessions for some were the least liked by others. The differences in preference may have been down to personality, but in one group at least, it also seemed to relate to gender, with the men preferring a robust approach and the women preferring something gentler and more subtle. This may not be true across the board, but it is worth paying attention to gender balance (and other factors of culture and ethnicity) when thinking about facilitators or guest speakers.

Giving the participants activities to do between sessions will help them to carry their learning over into the rest of their lives, engage with the material in greater depth and take responsibility for their own learning. We discovered the hard way that it is not a good idea to refer to these activities as 'homework', as this term has negative connotations for many people.

What?

What resources need to be in place before you begin?

Suddenly I realised – two people isn't enough. You need backup. If there are only two people, and someone drops off the edge, then you're on your own. Two isn't a large enough number. You need three at least.[18]

Even though at least two of you will be involved in facilitating the course, it's important to have some further support, specifically in the areas of prayer and supervision. It's good to ask for this work to be remembered as part of regular church services or pastoral team meetings, but you may also want to set up a small group who will specifically pray for this project either as a virtual network or by meeting together.

It's also advisable to make contact with someone who has expertise in the area of death and dying, perhaps a health care professional or hospital or hospice chaplain, who is willing to be available at the end of a phone in case you run into unexpected difficulties.

It's likely you will want to invite some additional speakers for certain sessions, for example a palliative care practitioner, a funeral director, or a solicitor. Make contact with them well in advance to ensure that you can get to know them a little and so that they will have a clear understanding of what you are asking them to do. It's usually advisable to put this in writing; it's easy for busy people to forget the precise details of what's required for a particular occasion and then just revert to their usual spiel, which may not fit the bill for your specific situation.

If you're planning to play music (which is almost certain), make sure you have equipment that will work in your chosen venue and check you have copyright to use it. If you're planning some artwork, you'll need to budget for and obtain some materials. It's important that these are new rather than stuff you have leftover in the cupboard.

There's a lot of free published material available, and it's being updated all the time (see links on pp. 145–46). As many older people do not have ready access to the internet it's a good idea to download or send off in advance for printed versions of the literature you may want to use.

What are the underlying themes of the whole course?

The sessions should include material on:

- Looking back and letting go
- Savouring life now
- Looking forward in hope

Looking back and letting go
Preparing well for death involves a delicate balance between staying in control and letting go. This balance is something that we all struggle with, and it will change depending on where we are on our 'death trajectory'. Your course should raise early on the prospect of beginning to let go of things in this life. The most concrete way of doing this is deciding to make a will, but there are other ways of 'putting one's affairs in order.' These include drawing the various threads of one's life together to weave a coherent story, and also dealing with unfinished business (be it pleasant or painful) in relationships.

Just as we are usually advised to update our wills every ten years, we also need to do some regular updating of the story of our lives. For a younger person it may feel as if there are many chapters left to come. Surprisingly, this may also be true for an older person, especially if he or she believes that life continues after death. For other older or terminally ill people there is a real sense that the story is moving to a close; one older person whispered to me hours before his death, 'And we all lived happily ever after.' He had literally completed the story of his (earthly) life.

Savouring life
But we should live fully until we die. So it's important to support people in inhabiting the present with gratitude and with a sense that they can continue to grow as human beings right up to the end of their lives. There are practical and active ways to do this, but it can also be about reframing the way we see things. For example, very old or chronically sick people can feel as if they are just marking time in a waiting room, yet this period of life can yield unforeseen treasures. Bodily losses and hardship, painful as they undoubtedly are, can make people spiritually more aware as they focus on the essentials of life. And as this life draws towards its end there can be a sense of standing poised at the threshold of something new; for some this feels so real that they can almost see and touch it. As discussed on p. 21, it's as if a spiritual mountaintop has been reached that offers vistas unseen by most people. It affirms the value of people – young or old – who are in their last years, months, or days as people of special wisdom and insight.

If your group is made up of frail or very old people you might like to explore this idea with them, helping them to value and voice their experiences.

Looking forward
Planning for a time when one no longer has capacity to make decisions (usually done through a lasting power of attorney) is wise, and your course can draw this to people's attention and show them how to take the first steps. Planning one's funeral both helps in the process of facing up to what is coming and (if not over-prescriptive) can be a gift to those left behind.

While death is ultimately uncontrollable, we are fortunate in the UK to have the right to make informed choices about our dying. However, our reticence in talking about death can make this a daunting prospect. Your course can begin to open up conversations about the options available and how to communicate personal wishes to medical staff and loved ones. These conversations should not just be about physical and social care but also about spiritual care.

Finally, our research has found that people are eager to talk about what happens after death. They have many questions, hopes and fears. Even if they have been faithful Christians for many years their thoughts will not always fit neatly into textbook Christian theology, but they should not be dismissed for that. Helping people to explore their ideas about life and death and to make connections with the Christian story is one of the most exciting aspects of running this sort of course.

The sessions

Session 1: Be prepared

Welcome and introduction (15 mins)

Begin the session by introducing yourself and offering words of welcome. Explain what the course is about. It's helpful to have this written down. There is a flyer which explains what the course is about on page 142.

It may also be helpful to begin by reading a poem. Choose one suitable to your participants and avoid highly religious or sentimental poems. The idea is simply to get the subject on the table, not to communicate deep truths or religious dogma.

We have used 'The gifts of death' by Connie Barlow[19] and Joan Walsh Anglund's very brief poem 'The miracle of life'.[20]

In their different ways these communicate the reality of death but also frame it as something natural, and they contain within them seeds of hope.

Invite any initial reflections on the poem but do not offer your own.

Explain that the focus in this first session is looking forward and preparing. For older generations prudence was seen as a virtue; being well prepared for future eventualities is easily recognised as wise by people over 60. This is not so much the case with younger people and may need more in the way of discussion.

Making a will and lasting power of attorney (40 mins)

Have a short presentation on making a will and invite participants to ask questions or share experiences. Remind participants that 'You can't take it with you' and introduce the idea of letting go well. Reflect on the way that people can dispose of their worldly goods in a way that ensures peace between those left behind rather than sowing discord and conflict that may persist for generations. It's likely that some of your participants will have first-hand experience of this that they may wish to share. Address the tricky issue of who to choose as executor; make it clear that this doesn't have to be a family member, and indeed it can be helpful to have an executor who has a bit of emotional distance. This can be a liberating discovery for some people who are caught up in unhelpful family dynamics. The executor needs to be named in the will, and when it is finally signed this must be witnessed by two people who are not beneficiaries and who also need to sign it. It is advisable (though not legally required) to have help from a solicitor when making a will.

Most people are reasonably familiar with the process of making a will, but 'Lasting Power of Attorney' (LPA) may need more in the way of explanation. An LPA is a document in which you authorise two or more named individuals to act in your interests in the event that you become 'incapable'.[21] The individuals acting for you are called 'attorneys'. You can make an LPA for decisions about your property and finances OR about your health and general welfare. It's advisable for LPAs to be drawn up by a solicitor, but you can do it yourself online.[22] It needs to be registered with the Public Guardian and this will involve paying a fee.[23]

It's desirable that this presentation on wills and LPAs is given by an invited expert. Whether you use an expert or try and do it yourself, you should make sure that you have up-to-date accessible literature on these topics available for your participants to take away. The Law Society, Age UK and the Alzheimer's Society are the best sources.

Conclusion (5 mins)

Introduce participants to the idea of carrying out an activity in preparation for the next session. In order to transition from the idea of letting go of possessions into the area of life stories, invite participants to consider two questions:

1. How would you like to be remembered by people after you have died?
2. What gem of wisdom would you like to pass on to those left behind?

Finish with a prayer, if appropriate.

Session 2: The story of my life

Welcome (2–3 mins)

Begin the session by welcoming any newcomers and briefly reminding participants of what was covered in the previous session.

Move into the topic by suggesting that part of living well in our last days is to go about the task of drawing all the threads of our life story together, to reflect on what it was all about and, from the perspective of a whole life lived, to ask again the question, 'Who am I?'

Identity discussion (20 mins)

Remind the participants of the questions they were asked to consider at the end of the previous session (it may help to have these written out on a flip chart). Depending on the size of your group you may want to ask participants to break into smaller groups of about half a dozen to discuss the first question. After 10 minutes or so reconvene to gather responses; then repeat the procedure for the second question.

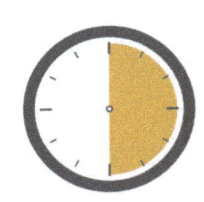

Creative response (30 mins)

There are various ways of working creatively with the themes that emerge:

> Making a wisdom tree, using a branch as a framework and tying paper leaves with participants' responses written on them. This would make a good prayer installation for a church or a school.
>
> Writing a 'gratitude' letter to someone who has made a difference in participants' lives but whom they have never had a chance to thank. Knowing you have made a difference is one of the things that gives people satisfaction at the end of life. The letter might be posted or simply written and kept (and this will clearly be necessary if the individual concerned has already died). It could form a focus for personal prayer. You might provide 'Thank you' cards for this purpose. Consider a similar exercise with 'Sorry' cards; this would obviously be more emotionally demanding and is probably best offered as an exercise participants might pursue in their own time.
>
> Inviting participants to write an epitaph or create a design for their headstone. This was tried very successfully in 2017 when the artist Alan Kane invited ten young people between the ages of 15 and 18 to develop proposals for their own headstones. They responded thoughtfully and playfully, producing poignant and often humorous designs. The result was the 'Early Graves' exhibition at the Royal Shakespeare Company in Stratford-upon-Avon.
>
> Making memory boxes. You could either share memory boxes made by the facilitators as examples, or the previous week you

> could have asked participants to bring one item that they would like to put in a memory box and invite them to speak about this. There will not be time for every participant to make and share a whole memory box in the session, but you should consider this as a separate activity, perhaps as a follow up to your group. It is an ideal activity for adults and children to do together. Here are some instructions:
>
>> The box should be large enough to accommodate several items but not too large to carry around. A large shoe box is about the right size. The box can be covered in a decoration that expresses something about those making it. The contents should be a variety of objects that signify important parts of the life of the individual or community. It is useful to include a short written explanation of the items… My experience of sharing memory boxes in a group is that we quickly establish intimacy with each other. People who think they know each other well are surprised to find out new and significant things about their companions… Memory boxes can also be a precious legacy for those left behind… The box can give a sense of what 'Grandma was really like.' I know one woman in her fifties who insisted on including a pair of black silk stockings in her memory box. This was so that any future grandchildren who knew her only as frail and forgetful would understand that she had in earlier days been a vibrant, sexy and sensual woman, and that this was also part of her story.[24]

Reflection on the session (5 mins)

Before you finish the session make sure you devote a few minutes to drawing out some themes and reflecting on them. Try and turn the session itself into a story by summarising what was done and said. One helpful image of living life well is that of weaving a tapestry out of many different threads, so that they are not tangled or left hanging but come together in a unique and beautiful way. This weaving should go on throughout our life, but in its final years it naturally becomes more intense. This is an image that works particularly well in my community of Witney whose identity is strongly connected with blanket-weaving. You may find that you are able to come up with an image that makes special sense in your own setting.

Depending on the faith and personalities of your participants, you may wish to bring this natural image into conversation with the Christian story. You might ask if God is part of the story or tapestry and, if so, how? You might want to speak of God knowing our whole story (Psalm 139), calling us by name (Isaiah 43:1–3) or knowing us as unique individuals (Isaiah 49:15–16). Make sure this part of the session stays more like a conversation than a sermon.

Conclusion (2–3 mins)

Finally, invite participants to carry out two activities, both linking the idea of identity with the funeral, in preparation for the next session:

1. Bring a reading that you would like at your funeral
2. Think about this question: 'Who is my funeral for?'

Finish with a prayer, if appropriate.

Session 3: Planning my funeral

Welcome (2–3 mins)

Begin the session by welcoming any newcomers (this is probably the latest point at which people could join the course) and briefly reminding participants of what was covered in the previous session. Try and link the idea of identity with the task of planning one's funeral, and also loop back to the idea of balancing letting go with being in control.

What (and who) is a funeral for? (10 mins)

It's helpful for participants to think about whether the funeral is primarily a means of asserting their identity – 'This was/is me!' – or whether it's really to help those left behind to say goodbye, or whether it is something else altogether – a handing over of the deceased into the care of God. Perhaps it's all of these, and they need to be held together.

Choosing hymns and poems (20 mins)

Divide into smaller groups of three or so and ask participants to share their choices of funeral poems with each other. If some have not brought poems they could talk about a favourite hymn (it's helpful to have hymn books to hand), or you may wish to provide some copies of poems that are often used for funerals. These are readily available on the internet and there are also some good published anthologies.[25]

Funeral practicalities (25 mins)

You may then wish to have a funeral director give a Q&A session about current options for funerals, including pre-paid financial packages. Alternatively, you may choose to talk people through the funeral service for your denomination yourself, especially if you're very experienced in taking funerals, and simply give participants written resources from a range of funeral providers.

Conclusion (2–3 mins)

Explain clearly that the next session will be on the actual process of dying, and invite participants between now and then to reflect on the question 'What is a good death?'

Finish with a prayer, if appropriate.

Session 4: The last days

Welcome and setting the scene (5 mins)

Begin the session by briefly reminding participants of what was covered in the previous session, again stressing the tension between being in control and letting go. Explain that this session will be on the actual process of dying. Depending on the make-up of your group, you may wish to read:

> *In the last days it will be, God declares, that I will pour out my Spirit upon all flesh, and your sons and your daughters shall prophesy, and your young men shall see visions, and your old men shall dream dreams.*
> ACTS 2:17)

This reading is a way of offering the idea that the end of earthly life can be seen as a place of spiritual blessing. Nevertheless, dying is physically rigorous, and if this session is to explore it well its raw physicality must be acknowledged. Providing a holding environment will be particularly important in this session.

Next, move into the subject of the session by saying that as death approaches we move from a natural feeling of wanting to be in control of things to a readiness to let go. Of course, we are right to wish for good control of any pain and discomfort, and to be in a safe and secure place with loved ones close at hand. Today, more than ever, there's a very good chance that this is indeed what we will experience. Palliative care practice has come on in leaps and bounds in recent years, and patients now have a good deal of choice and control over where they end their days and what sort of treatment and care they wish to have. This is all part of 'a good death.'

Q&A session with palliative care professional(s) (25 mins)

For this session it's wise to have an invited speaker who is a palliative care expert and who knows the services in your locality. Ask him or her to talk about choices for where to spend one's final days (at home, in a hospice, or a community hospital etc.), options for medical treatment at this time, how to make things as pleasant as possible and accessing spiritual care. Much of this will be specific to your local area. If the group feels a safe enough space, participants may feel emboldened to ask questions about the process of dying itself and what it might feel like. This may be a particular issue for participants who have witnessed the death of a loved one that has not appeared peaceful.

Living wills (25 mins)

As part of this session you should discuss Advance Decisions (essentially 'living wills'). In an Advance Decision the individual sets out his or her wishes in the event that s/he becomes incapacitated and unable to communicate them directly. These wishes are usually related to medical interventions during the last days that may prolong life but not increase its quality, for example aggressive resuscitation after cardiac arrest; feeding through a tube when the individual is unconscious; giving antibiotics for pneumonia. It can also include wishes on organ donation after death.

Advance Decisions are explained on the NHS website: nhs.uk/conditions/end-of-life-care/planning-ahead/advance-decision-to-refuse-treatment.

It's advisable to talk to one's GP about the process of making an Advance Decision, and several organisations (most notably Compassion in Dying produce forms and guidance). The written record can be placed in the individual's medical notes, but copies can also be made available to loved ones. There's a UK-wide scheme (probably taken up more in some parts of the country than others) called 'Message in a Bottle' in which the individual's wishes are placed in an easily identifiable container kept in the fridge. This scheme is organised by the Lions' Clubs. For more information see: lionsclubs.co/MemberArea/home/lions-message-in-a-bottle.

It is very important to be clear that a Living Will/Advance Decision cannot be used to request assisted dying, which is currently illegal in the UK.[26] This may be an area of confusion for participants, not helped by the fact that the two key campaign groups on the two questions have similar names ('Compassion in Dying' for Advance Decisions, and 'Dignity in Dying' for assisted dying). See FAQs (p. 130).

Formal Advance Decisions are only a part of the more general process of Advance Care Planning, in which the individual thinks through and discusses his or her wishes relating to the end of life with loved ones and health and social care professionals (for example care of any pets that may outlive them). It may well be appropriate for a faith practitioner such as a vicar or chaplain to be part of this process, so that spiritual needs at the time of death are not forgotten. An example of the sort of thing that might be included would be, 'If I am found unconscious please call my parish priest on this number...' (You should provide an opportunity to go into spiritual care around the time of death in more detail in the next session, but flag it up here.)

As the discussion draws to a close, you may wish to reflect on the idea that dying is in many ways like giving birth. It's wise and reassuring to have a birth plan, but sometimes events take over and labour is not fully controllable. It is also wise and reassuring to have a death plan, but at the end of the day we should acknowledge that death is not fully controllable either.

Conclusion (5 mins)

Invite participants to prepare for the next session which will be entitled 'Departing in peace'. (It's a good idea to mention the word 'peace' at this point as it will signal the move from talking about potentially disturbing issues to a place of relative calm.) There are two possible activities for the next session, and which you choose will depend on the nature of your group. The first option is to share participants' choices of music to 'go out to' – what they would like to hear in their final days and hours. In this case invite participants to bring the music with them (or at least to let you know in advance so that you can try and source it). The second is to have a 'bucket list' discussion; what things do they feel they need to have done in order to depart in peace? In this case invite participants to come with ideas and stories appropriate to the task.

Finish with a prayer, if appropriate.

Session 5: Departing in peace

Welcome and setting the scene (15 mins)

Begin the session by briefly reminding participants of what was covered in the previous session, making the link between a good death and departing in peace. Read Simeon's song:

> *Lord, now lettest thou thy servant depart in peace according to thy word. For mine eyes have seen thy salvation, which thou hast prepared before the face of all people; to be a light to lighten the Gentiles and to be the glory of thy people Israel.*
> LUKE 2:29–32 (BCP)

Reflect on the fact that Simeon had a strong sense of what he would need to have seen and done in order to depart in peace. Note that this was not primarily about looking back or about thinking about himself, but about looking to the future and the needs of others – in fact the whole world. Simeon is seeing deep meaning and purpose in things, and so he can leave this life content. Note also that we are not told what age Simeon was; it's possible that he was a young or middle-aged man, so his song can apply to people of all ages facing death.

To set the scene further, you may wish to play all or part of the very beautiful aria 'Schlummert ein, ihr matten Augen' ('Rest weary eyes') from J.S. Bach's setting of Simeon's song, Ich Habe Genug ('I have enough') BWV 82: **youtube.com/watch?v=QioNzrN9wdI**.

Spiritual care at the time of death (15 mins)

Talk to participants about what the Christian church offers in the last days. If some of your participants are of other faith traditions it will be important to acknowledge this and point them in the direction of someone to talk to from their own tradition, but they may still be interested in what Christians do; you should not be ashamed of the clearly faith-based aspect of the course. In the Church of England, this is set out in the *Common Worship Pastoral Services* book section 'Ministry at the time of death'.[27] You may want to have some copies of the prayers, particularly those for 'Laying on of hands and anointing' and 'Commendation' available for participants to read and take away (or the equivalent from your own denomination). These are deeply comforting and go some way to dispelling anxieties evoked by terms such as 'Last rites' and 'Extreme unction'.

At this point you may wish to draw any local volunteer end-of-life befriending schemes to the attention of your participants. (The availability of these varies across the country and you will need to do some of your own research into this. Contacting your local hospice is a good place to start).

Bucket list OR 'music to go out to' (25 mins)

For both of these you will need to allow those participants who wish to, to tell something of their own story without one person dominating the group. You will also need to draw out some common themes as you sum up the session. For example, when we facilitated one 'music to go out to' session we noticed that several of the chosen pieces were like lullabies (as is 'Schlummert ein'), some evoked childhood memories and some soared high, evoking bird flight. This led to a brief reflection on dying as being respectively like going to sleep, like going home at last and a liberation of the human spirit.

Conclusion (2–3 mins)

Invite participants to prepare for the next session by considering the question of what happens after we die (if anything).

Finish with a prayer, if appropriate.

Session 6: What comes next?

Welcome (5 mins)

Begin by saying that the question mark in the title of this session is important. None of us has gone through death and come out the other side, so all our statements about it are conjecture, some more informed than others. The Bible itself speaks with many voices on this issue. The New Testament is based on a rock-solid belief in the raising of Christ; it nevertheless offers a multifaceted account made up of many separate images, none of which does full justice to the reality of the resurrection life. This remains deeply mysterious territory.

Creative activities and reflection (40 mins)

This session aims to give participants permission to advance tentative, provisional ideas and images, hopes and fears, rather than giving them all the answers. You might think of this as hearing their stories so that you can bring these into conversation with God's story. There are a number of ways of doing this and you should be guided by the needs of your particular group.

You could use various forms of visual art media – collage, paints, pastels etc.; alongside this you might also offer participants the opportunity to write poetry (what one person referred to as 'my painting in words'). Another way is to engage with the Death and Life reflection cards (available from **brfonline.org.uk/death-and-life-cards**). These place biblical themes alongside a variety of images to encourage individual reflection or discussion in small groups of two or three.

The session should have an even balance between creative or reflective activity and input from the facilitator(s). Your input should be to explore questions raised, affirm the ideas and images generated and link them with aspects of the Christian tradition.

Facilitating reflection
The way human beings think about death seems to fit recurring themes. Some of these are therefore likely to come up in the activity and discussion. Some may have come up already in earlier sessions, and so you may be able to make helpful links back across the whole course:

> Dying as a kind of labour, and therefore death as a kind of rebirth;
>
> Death as a final, well-deserved, peaceful sleep;
>
> Death as going home;
>
> Death as the next phase in the deceased's journey: a pilgrimage, a heroic quest, another chance to right wrongs;
>
> Death as a return to the place from where the deceased first came: the stars, the earth, parents or ancestors;
>
> Death as liberation from captivity.

We find such metaphors – commonly expressed in poetry, music and images from nature such as clouds, the greening of spring, or the flight of winged creatures – plausible even in the face of the self-evident bodily decay of the deceased. Part of the human process of grief seems to involve an attunement to the presence of the deceased in certain natural forms and creatures.

A moving example of this sort of instinct at work is given by the writer Paul Heiney in account of his sea voyages in the period following the loss of his son, Nicholas, at the age of 23:

> *Sailing out from Mar del Plata three days later, a snowy white bird – possibly a tern – circled overhead. I watched it power through the disturbed air in the lee of the mainsail before soaring high, then swooping, almost to land on my head. Round and round it flew, never leaving me, as if wanting to play.*
>
> *I will try to be neither superstitious nor sentimental about this, but in the dark days after Nicholas's death I watched the regular visits of such a white bird as it hovered over the place where he died... It flew in tight circles, riding the thermals of a summer afternoon, then swooping towards me so close that often I ducked; then back it went to that tragic spot, soaring and diving, holding my attention with such a force that I have no idea how long I watched its antics. Then it was gone. I would have thought no more of it if it had not reappeared the next day, and the day after that.*[28]

Heiney goes on to describe how the visits of the bird became less frequent (or perhaps he noticed them less) as his acute grief subsided.

Bringing such human experiences and any accompanying beliefs into conversation with the Christian faith requires sensitivity and respect, and it can be challenging. Orthodox Christian teaching certainly does not support the idea of the transmigration of spirits in any simple sense. In fact, Christian teaching on life after death is difficult for most people to connect with at an intuitive level. It essentially states that immediately on death human beings go to a place of rest where they are in communion with the Godhead; their biological bodies decay, but they continue to exist; on the last day, when Christ appears in glory and heaven is married with earth, those who are in Christ rise with new eternal bodies; then there is some sort of judgment by Christ. It is very difficult to marry such bald dogmatic statements with personally compelling experiences like those of Heiney.

There is, however, more leverage in the area of images and poetry. The Bible is full of birds, including birds as metaphors for the human spirit and the divine Spirit. So at least some points of connection can be identified and resonances drawn out. For example:

O that I had wings like a dove! I would fly away and be at rest; truly, I would flee far away; I would lodge in the wilderness; I would hurry to find a shelter for myself from the raging wind and tempest.
PSALM 55:6–8

How lovely is your dwelling place, O Lord of hosts! My soul longs, indeed it faints for the courts of the Lord; my heart and my flesh sing for joy to the living God. Even the sparrow finds a home, and the swallow a nest for herself, where she may lay her young, at your altars, O Lord of hosts, my King and my God. Happy are those who live in your house, ever singing your praise.
PSALM 84:1–4

In those days Jesus came from Nazareth of Galilee and was baptised by John in the Jordan. And just as he was coming up out of the water, he saw the heavens torn apart and the Spirit descending like a dove on him. And a voice came from heaven, 'You are my Son, the Beloved; with you I am well pleased.'
MARK 1:9–11)

[Jesus] also said, 'With what can we compare the kingdom of God, or what parable will we use for it? It is like a mustard seed, which, when sown upon the ground, is the smallest of all the seeds on earth; yet when it is sown it grows up and becomes the greatest of all shrubs, and puts forth large branches, so that the birds of the air can make nests in its shade.'
MARK 4: 30–32

Along with texts such as these, the traditional Christian iconography of angels is also very important here. Angels are (winged) heavenly messengers who come into their own at points where heaven touches earth, and who offer a natural bridge between folk spirituality and the Christian gospel. It's not uncommon for a prematurely deceased individual to be idealised and asserted to be an angel. While this idea is, again, at odds with orthodox Christian teaching, it's a serious attempt to make sense of loss and manage grief, and should be worked with sensitively; the underlying instinct that the deceased has achieved fulfilment through profound transformation is sound and can be affirmed.

This brief indicative example is focused on birds and other winged creatures. Hopefully, you will be able to develop it further and also do something similar in relation to some of the other common human ideas and images for death.

Some FAQs

One cannot anticipate every question asked or issue raised in this session, but here are some suggestions for engaging with some of the more frequent and difficult ones:

Will I see my loved ones again in the next life?
While Jesus' words about the resurrection indicate that things will be profoundly different (Matthew 22:29–30), he does not say that we will be separated from our loved ones. Paul says that we will be 'together with them' (1 Thessalonians 4:17) at Christ's second coming, precisely because he does not want his readers to 'grieve as others do who have no hope' (v. 13). It may be helpful to tell a widow(er) that the marriage service words 'till death us do part' were probably originally 'till death us depart', and do not signify a final separation.

Am I/was my loved one good enough to face my maker just as we are?
This worry lies behind the resurgence of interest in the mediaeval notion of purgatory or related ideas about a process of continuing self-improvement after death, neither of which have biblical support. It may be helpful to stress the idea of 'faith not works' to Christians who are familiar with this idea. More broadly, the emphasis of the gospel is on God's seeking out those who are lost more than their finding their way to him (Luke 19:10); Luke 15 offers a valuable way of exploring this. The incident of the thief on the cross (Luke 23:42–43) tells us that at the end of life the most unlikely people can do private business with God of which we are unaware. This may be a great comfort to those who have been praying for a change of heart in a loved one with little obvious effect.

My loved one died by suicide – where is s/he?
There is an ancient Christian tradition that in the darkness of Holy Saturday Jesus descended to preach to the 'spirits in prison' (1 Peter 3:19; see also Matthew 12:40; Ephesians 4:9). It is referred to in the Apostles' Creed and was the basis of the mediaeval idea of the 'harrowing of hell'. Whatever we make of this, it opens up the vitally important notion that there is nowhere so dark and wretched that it is beyond the redeeming reach of God in Christ. Here is a link to a rather cheerful depiction of this which you may like to use: thevcs.org/x/christ-hymn/harrowing-hell-from.

Is there a hell and, if so, who goes there?
There's no getting away from the fact that Jesus talked about hell in very vivid terms. However, his words are always in the context of God's ultimate judgement of those in power who have exploited or neglected the weak (Matthew 18:23–35; Luke 16:19–31; Mark 9:42–48). It is all about God's justice. This is actually a comfort to those who have suffered injustice and abuse at the hands of those who are now deceased. The parable of the wheat and the tares (Matthew 13:24–30) tells us that we cannot know what the final reckoning will involve other than that it will be fair, and so it's not good for us to judge or speculate. What we do know is that Christ will recognise his own, and that this will include 'other sheep that do not belong to this fold' (John 10:16). You may find it helpful to

refer participants to C.S. Lewis' *The Last Battle* if they wish to explore this further.

What about stillborn babies and late miscarriages?
Jesus said 'Let the little children come to me; do not stop them; for it is to such as these that the kingdom of God belong.' (Mark 10:14). He did not qualify this statement with a demand for baptism. The New Testament is clear: infants have a special place in the heart of God.

Is it okay to pray for deceased loved ones?
This question is more likely to come from people from a Protestant background who may have been brought up to believe that praying for the dead is a like the mediaeval practice of saying masses to get them through purgatory quicker, yet find that they have a great desire to pray for those they love and see no more. It may be helpful to explain that intercession is turning to God with people on our heart and, as our loved ones do not cease to exist at death, it makes sense to pray for them too. If we believe that they are already in some sort of communion with God we can also pray *with* them as part of the 'communion of saints.' Within the Eucharist the Sanctus – 'with angels and archangels, and with all the company of heaven,' – can become a focus for this, as can All Saints' Day.

Why didn't God heal my loved one(s) even though I prayed faithfully?
It is both good and natural to pray for the physical cure of someone we love but at some point prayers may need to shift towards praying for a good death. This is part of letting go and acknowledging that death is the earthly destination for everyone. After all, every person who was healed in the Bible died eventually (even Lazarus).

What about assisted dying?
There are profound disagreements about this issue both within the church and in wider society. The theological arguments against it rest on the idea that life is a gift from God (Genesis 2:7) and that only God can take it back through natural processes, it is not ours to give back. The theological arguments in favour of it rest on the idea that God is compassionate and is not in the business of burdening his people (Luke 11:46; Matthew 11:28–30). An open attitude to the issue is pastorally appropriate, even if you have strong personal views. If a vulnerable person raises this question, it is wise to probe further as there may be safeguarding implications.

You may find that one or more members of your group are keen to discuss issues around assisted dying further. This should not distract from the main focus of the session, so you may need to have a separate pastoral conversation. If you do this, it will be helpful to consult a web-based resource constructed by the University of Cardiff called 'Christian perspectives on death and dying'. It covers both Advance Decisions and assisted dying: xerte.cardiff.ac.uk/play_5767.

But, if you think you are likely to be out of your depth it is advisable simply to explain this and direct the individual(s) to the resource.

Conclusion (15 mins)

This session is the most open of all, yet it comes at the end of the course and so attention must be paid to good closure. Draw the discussion to a close and consider asking individual participants to read out the texts from the reflection cards. Even if you don't do this, make sure that you finish by reading this extract from Revelation:

> *God himself will be with them and be their God; he will wipe every tear from their eyes. Death will be no more; mourning and crying and pain will be no more, for the first things have passed away.*
> REVELATION 21:1–4

Finish the course with your usual prayer, if appropriate. You may wish to add a final farewell by using the words of the Grace (2 Corinthians 13:13). If you are in a more 'catholic' setting it may be good to end with 'May the souls of the faithful departed, through the mercy of God, rest in peace.' To which the response is, 'and rise in glory.'

During the post-session period while refreshments are being shared, it is a good idea to ask participants to complete a simple evaluation form. See pages 133–34.

Well-Prepared course: evaluation

Thank you for attending this course.

It would be very helpful if you could let us know how you found it by answering the questions below:

How many sessions were you able to attend?

1	2	3	4	5	6

To what extent has attending the course

Made you more confident about issues around death and dying?

Not at all	To a small extent	To a moderate extent	To a great extent

Deepened or enriched your personal faith?

Not at all	To a small extent	To a moderate extent	To a great extent

PLEASE TURN OVER

What were the most helpful aspects of the course?

_____
_____
_____
_____

What were the least helpful aspects of the course?

_____
_____
_____
_____

Are there things that you would like to have been included?

_____
_____
_____
_____

Do you have any further comments or suggestions?

_____
_____
_____
_____

THANK YOU FOR YOUR TIME

Preparation exercises for facilitators

1 Remember a time

This should take about ten minutes but you should allow some time before to find a quiet place where you won't be disturbed and to be still. You will need to allow some time afterwards to come back into the land of the living.

Recall a memorable experience that you have had in relation to death and dying. Choose a specific event that lasted from a few moments up to a few hours, not a general set of experiences.

Write about this as if you were talking to a good friend. Describe what happened, when and where it happened, and what you were thinking and feeling at the time. You may also want to add some reflections that emerged afterwards.

2 Be aware of your attitude towards death

The questionnaire on the following pages is a version of a research tool called the 'Death Attitudes Profile – Revised'.[29] It consists of a number of statements related to different attitudes towards death. The overall score isn't important, but filling in the questionnaire should make you more aware of your attitude to death. Read each statement carefully and then indicate the extent to which you agree or disagree by circling the appropriate statement.

3 Reflect on a Bible passage

Choose a phrase or verse from the Bible that sums up your hope in the face of death, for example 'with the Lord forever', 'life in its fullness', 'then we will see face to face', 'do not be afraid: you are worth more than many sparrows'. Reflect prayerfully on why it is precious to you.

1. Death is no doubt a grim experience

Strongly disagree	Moderately disagree	Undecided	Moderately agree	Strongly agree

2. The prospect of my own death arouses anxiety in me

Strongly disagree	Moderately disagree	Undecided	Moderately agree	Strongly agree

3. I avoid thoughts of death at all costs

Strongly disagree	Moderately disagree	Undecided	Moderately agree	Strongly agree

4. I believe that I will be in heaven after I die

Strongly disagree	Moderately disagree	Undecided	Moderately agree	Strongly agree

5. Death will bring an end to all my troubles

Strongly disagree	Moderately disagree	Undecided	Moderately agree	Strongly agree

6. Death should be viewed as a natural, undeniable and unavoidable event

Strongly disagree	Moderately disagree	Undecided	Moderately agree	Strongly agree

7. I am disturbed by the finality of death

Strongly disagree	Moderately disagree	Undecided	Moderately agree	Strongly agree

8. Death is an entrance to a place of ultimate satisfaction

Strongly disagree	Moderately disagree	Undecided	Moderately agree	Strongly agree

9. Death provides an escape from this terrible world

Strongly disagree	Moderately disagree	Undecided	Moderately agree	Strongly agree

10. Whenever the thought of death enters my mind I try to push it away

Strongly disagree	Moderately disagree	Undecided	Moderately agree	Strongly agree

11. Death is deliverance from pain and suffering

Strongly disagree	Moderately disagree	Undecided	Moderately agree	Strongly agree

12. I always try not to think about death

Strongly disagree	Moderately disagree	Undecided	Moderately agree	Strongly agree

13. I believe that heaven will be a much better place than this world

Strongly disagree	Moderately disagree	Undecided	Moderately agree	Strongly agree

14. Death is a natural aspect of life

Strongly disagree	Moderately disagree	Undecided	Moderately agree	Strongly agree

15. Death is a union with God and eternal bliss

Strongly disagree	Moderately disagree	Undecided	Moderately agree	Strongly agree

16. Death brings a promise of a new and glorious life

Strongly disagree	Moderately disagree	Undecided	Moderately agree	Strongly agree

17. I would neither fear death nor welcome it

Strongly disagree	Moderately disagree	Undecided	Moderately agree	Strongly agree

18. I have an intense fear of death

Strongly disagree	Moderately disagree	Undecided	Moderately agree	Strongly agree

19. I avoid thinking about death altogether

Strongly disagree	Moderately disagree	Undecided	Moderately agree	Strongly agree

20. The subject of life after death troubles me greatly

Strongly disagree	Moderately disagree	Undecided	Moderately agree	Strongly agree

21. The fact that death will mean the end of everything as I know it frightens me

Strongly disagree	Moderately disagree	Undecided	Moderately agree	Strongly agree

22. I look forward to a reunion with my loved ones after I die

Strongly disagree	Moderately disagree	Undecided	Moderately agree	Strongly agree

23. I view death as a relief from earthly suffering

Strongly disagree	Moderately disagree	Undecided	Moderately agree	Strongly agree

24. Death is simply a part of the process of life

Strongly disagree	Moderately disagree	Undecided	Moderately agree	Strongly agree

25. I see death as a passage to an eternal and blessed place

Strongly disagree	Moderately disagree	Undecided	Moderately agree	Strongly agree

26. I try to have nothing to do with the subject of death

Strongly disagree	Moderately disagree	Undecided	Moderately agree	Strongly agree

27. Death offers a wonderful release of the soul

Strongly disagree	Moderately disagree	Undecided	Moderately agree	Strongly agree

28. One thing that gives me comfort in facing death is my belief in the afterlife

Strongly disagree	Moderately disagree	Undecided	Moderately agree	Strongly agree

29. I see death as a relief from the burdens of this life

Strongly disagree	Moderately disagree	Undecided	Moderately agree	Strongly agree

30. Death is neither good nor bad

Strongly disagree	Moderately disagree	Undecided	Moderately agree	Strongly agree

31. I look forward to life after death

Strongly disagree	Moderately disagree	Undecided	Moderately agree	Strongly agree

32. The uncertainty of not knowing what happens after death worries me

Strongly disagree	Moderately disagree	Undecided	Moderately agree	Strongly agree

Well-Prepared course

A six-week course on death and dying

As a society we're not good at talking about death, and as individuals we may try and avoid thinking about it. Yet as we get older it's natural for us to think more deeply about the issues that face us in our final years. We may:

> Look back over our lives and wonder if we have 'made a good job of things';
>
> Have some memories and wisdom we really want to pass on;
>
> Feel a need to make our peace with someone;
>
> Finally get around to making a will or thinking about our funeral.

We may also have some deeper questions about

> What 'the end' may be like for us;
>
> Whether it really is the end or the beginning of something better.

This short course provides a safe and pleasant space to discuss these issues. There will be discussion, music, poetry, art, spiritual reflection and refreshments.

This course is being run by:

VENUE:

TIME:

DATES:

If you would like to know more, please contact:

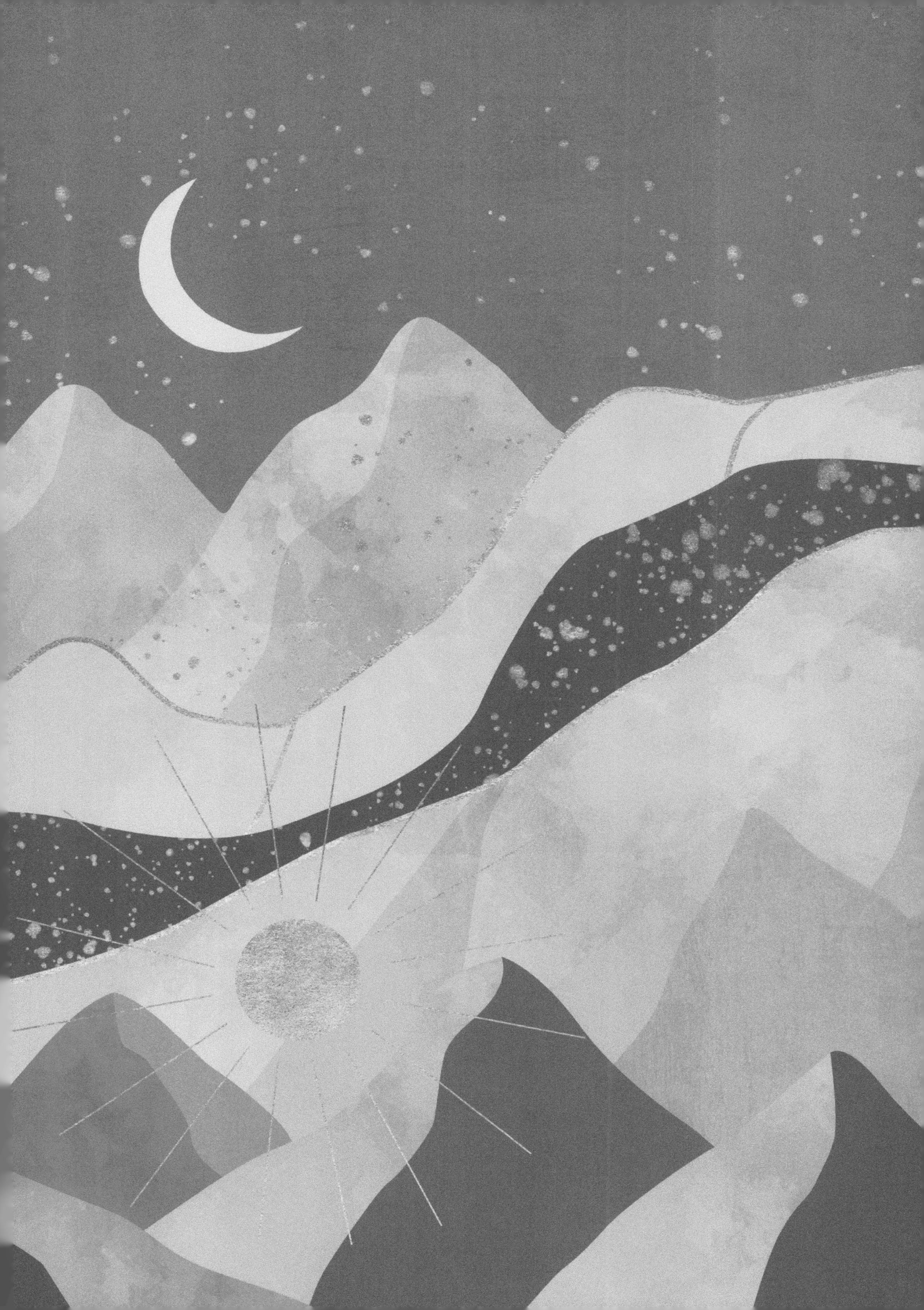

Background reading

Keith Albans and Malcolm Johnson (eds), *God, Me and Being Very Old: Stories of spirituality in later life* (SCM Press, 2013).

Paul Badham, *Making Sense Of Death and Immortality* (SPCK, 2013).

Sue Brayne, *The D Word: Talking about dying* (Continuum, 2010).

Marian Carter, *Dying to Live: A theological and practical workbook on death, dying and bereavement* (SCM, 2014).

Douglas Davies, *Death, Ritual and Belief: The rhetoric of funerary rites* (Cassell, 1997).

Douglas Davies, *The Theology of Death* (Bloomsbury, 2008).

Viktor Frankl, *Man's Search for Meaning* (Rider, new edition 2011).

Atul Gawande, *Being Mortal: Illness, medicine and what matters at the end* (Metropolitan Books, 2014).

Faith Gibson, *Reminiscence and Life Story Work: A practical guide* (Jessica Kingsley, 2011).

Philip Giddings, Martin Down, Elaine Sugden and Gareth Tuckwell, *Talking About Dying: Help in facing death and dying* (Wilberforce, 2016).

Paula Gooder, *Heaven* (SPCK, 2011).

Denise Inge, *A Tour of Bones: Facing fear and looking for life* (Bloomsbury. 2014).

Paul Kalanithi, *When Breath Becomes Air: What makes life living in the face of death* (Penguin, 2017).

Robert Kastenbaum, *The Psychology of Death* (Free Association, 2000).

Robert Kastenbaum, *On Our Way: The final passage through life and death* (University of California Press, 2004).

Allan Kellehear, *A Social History of Dying* (Cambridge University Press, 2007).

John S. Lampard, *Go Forth, Christian Soul: The biography of a prayer* (Wipf & Stock, 2015).

Elizabeth MacKinlay, *Aging, Spirituality and Palliative Care* (Haworth Pastoral Press, 2006).

Kathryn Mannix, *With the End in Mind: Dying, death and wisdom in an age of denial* (Collins, 2017).

Robert Neale, *The Art of Dying* (Harper & Rowe, 1971).

Jessica Rose and Michael Paterson (eds), *Enriching Ministry: Pastoral supervision in practice* (SCM, 2014).

Marianne Rozario and Lia Shimada, 'Ashes to Ashes: Beliefs, trends, and practices in dying, death, and the afterlife' (Theos and The Susanna Wesley Foundation, 2023).

Jeremy Taylor, *Holy Dying* (Forgotten Books, classic edition 2012, but several editions available).

The Archbishops' Council, *Grave Talk: Cards and facilitator's guide* (Church House Publishing, 2015).

Barbara Thompson and Robert Neimeyer (eds), *Grief and the Expressive Arts: Practices for creating meaning* (Routledge, 2014).

W.H. Vanstone, *The Stature of Waiting* (Darton, Longman & Todd, 2004).

Bob Wharton, *Voices from the Hospice: Staying with life through suffering and waiting* (SCM, 2015).

David Winter, *At the End of the Day: Enjoying life in the departure lounge* (BRF, 2013).

James Woodward, *Befriending Death* (SPCK, 2005).

Tom Wright, *Surprised by Hope* (SPCK, 2011).

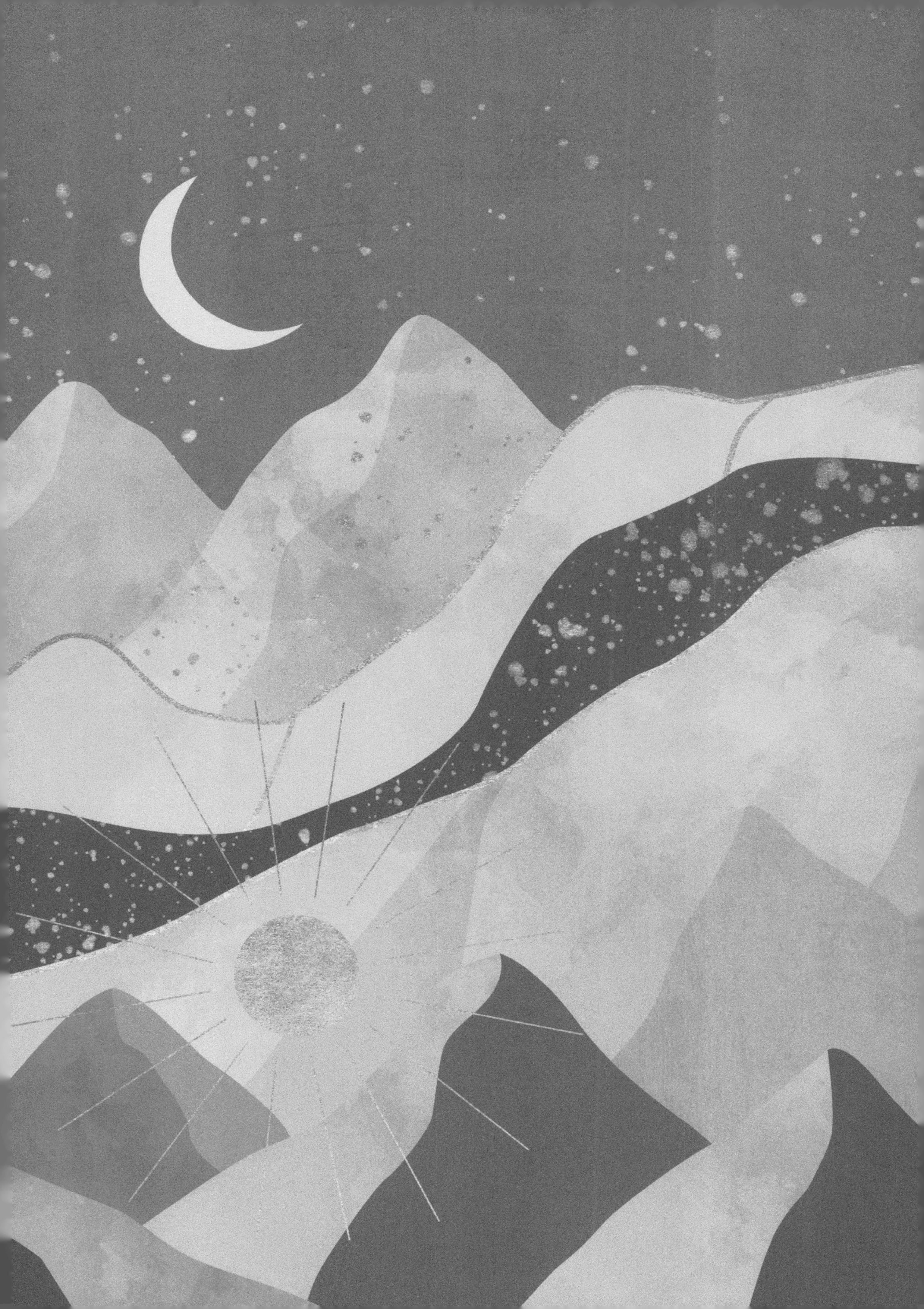

Acknowledgements

This work was funded in part by the Henry Smith Charity and we would like to express our thanks to Genevieve Ford-Saville and James Woodward for the part they played in this process. It was also part of the work of SCOP, the diocese of Oxford's initiative for the spiritual care of older people, and we are grateful to Bishop Michael Beasley for the support he gave at the planning stage.

It was overseen by a steering committee made up of Felicity Blair, Bishop Colin Fletcher, Sally Richards and Bishop Humphrey Southern who provided wise advice and direction.

Many clergy and lay people across Oxford Diocese helped with the research in various ways and we are particularly grateful to Phillip Tovey, David Knight and Polley Falconer for facilitating access to research participants.

Jeremy Brooks, Robert Glenny and Julie Mintern contributed greatly to the 'Living well' section through their thoughtful theological reflections.

Olivia Warburton and Debbie Thrower from BRF Ministries and Anna Chaplaincy have been greatly encouraging in the bringing together of the material in book form.

The original ideas for this work began to take shape during a period when Joanna Collicutt was a visiting fellow at the Oxford Institute for Population Ageing in 2011–12, and she is very grateful for their scholarly hospitality. The first piece of practical work involved a group of wonderful participants from churches in Witney, and their enthusiastic and deeply reflective responses inspired its further development.

Photographs are by Jo Ind and Rob Lainchbury.

Death and Life prayer

In the end,
We return
To the heart of matter.
To the heart of the matter:
That the love of God created us,
The spirit of God enlivened us,
And the mystery of God awaits us.
May the peace of God be with us
Now and forever.

Notes

1. From Theos 2023 report 'Ashes to Ashes: Beliefs, trends, and practices in dying, death and the afterlife': theosthinktank.co.uk/research/2023/04/12/ashes-to-ashes-beliefs-trends-and-practices-in-dying-death-and-the-afterlife.
2. Joanna Collicutt, 'Living in the end times: a short course addressing end of life issues for older people in an English parish church setting', *Working with Older People*, no. 19, vol. 3 (2015), pp. 140–49.
3. Victoria Slater and Joanna Collicutt, 'Living Well in the End Times (LWET): a project to research and support churches' engagement with issues of death and dying', *Practical Theology*, no. 11, vol. 2 (2018), pp. 176–88.
4. Quoted by Michael Barbato in Elizabeth Mackinlay, *Aging, Spirituality and Palliative Care* (Haworth Pastoral Press, 2006), p. 112.
5. W. H. Vanstone, *The Stature of Waiting: The pocket library of spiritual wisdom* (Darton, Longman & Todd, 2004).
6. Jeanne Sorrell, 'Listening in thin places: ethics in the care of persons with Alzheimer's disease', *Advances in Nursing Science*, no. 29, vol. 2 (2006), pp. 152–60.
7. Mark Oakley, *The Splash of Words: Believing in poetry* (Canterbury Press, 2016), p. xxiii.
8. Peter Gomes, *The Good Book: Reading the Bible with mind and heart* (Harper, 2002); see also Sorrell, 'Listening in thin places'.
9. See Douglas Davies, *The Theology of Death* (T&T Clark, 2008).
10. Abraham Maslow, *Motivation and Personality* (Harper, 1954).
11. N. T. Wright, 'On predestination and election': youtu.be/qKwIijhZW-M.
12. Vanstone, *The Stature of Waiting*, p. 67–68.
13. E. T. Cook and Alexander Wedderburn (eds), *Works of John Ruskin*, 39 vols (Longmans Green & Co., 1903–12), III, 34.
14. Cook and Wedderburn, *Works of John Ruskin*, III. 37–38
15. J. K. Rowling, *The Casual Vacancy* (Sphere, 2012).
16. For more ideas on making the most of churchyards, see caringforgodsacre.org.uk.
17. The exception to this is if a participant discloses a safeguarding-related issue. In this case, you should seek advice from your church safeguarding officer or, if that is not possible, from your local adult safeguarding board See scie.org.uk/care-act-2014/safeguarding-adults/safeguarding-adults-boards-checklist-and-resources/role-and-duties.asp.
18. *About a Boy* (2002), dir. Paul Weitz and Chris Weitz.
19. See huffingtonpost.com/rev-michael-dowd/a-scientific-honoring-of-death_b_1556839.html.
20. Joan Walsh Anglund, *A Slice of Snow* (Collins, 1970), p. 15.
21. This is a technical use of the word as found in the Mental Capacity Act of 2005.
22. See lastingpowerofattorney.service.gov.uk/home.
23. See gov.uk/government/organisations/office-of-the-public-guardian.
24. Joanna Collicutt, *Thinking of You: A resource for the spiritual care of people with dementia* (BRF, 2017), pp. 133–34.
25. Jeremy Brooks, *Heaven's Morning Breaks: Sensitive and practical reflections on funeral practice* (Kevin Mayhew, 2013); Mark Oakley, *Readings for funerals* (SPCK, 2015); Julia Watson, *Poems and Readings for Funerals* (Penguin, 2004).
26. See, for example The Commission for Assisted Dying, 'The current legal status of assisted dying is inadequate and incoherent…' (Demos, 2012): demos.co.uk/wp-content/uploads/2012/01/476_CoAD_FinalReport_158x240_I_web_single-NEW_.pdf.
27. The Archbishops' Council, *Common Worship Pastoral Services* (Church House Publishing, 2000), pp. 216–35: churchofengland.org/prayer-and-worship/worship-texts-and-resources/common-worship/death-and-dying/funeral.
28. Paul Heiney, *One Wild Song: A voyage in a lost son's wake* (Bloomsbury, 2015), pp. 109–10.
29. Paul Wong, Gary Reker and Gina Gesser, (1994). 'Death attitude profile – revised: a multidimensional measure of attitudes towards death' in Robert Neimeyer (ed.), *Death Anxiety Handbook: Research, instrumentation and application* (Taylor & Francis, 1994), pp. 121–48.

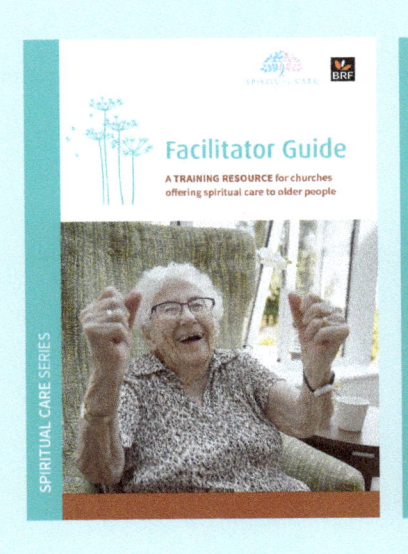

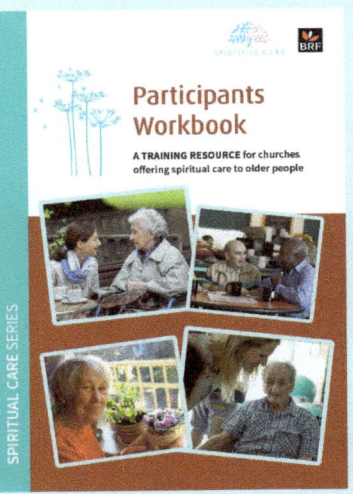

The Spiritual Care Series is an eight-week comprehensive course for churches who want to provide good quality spiritual care to older people in their local community. The course equips participants to understand the ageing process, supporting people to reconnect with their past and cope with the losses that ageing brings. It also covers the importance of good listening skills, communication and boundaries in the provision of this care.

Spiritual Care Series
Six-user bundle £360

annachaplaincy.org.uk/spiritual-care-series

When families experience bereavement and loss, it can be hard for the wider church community to know how best to support them. In this book, four experienced authors and practitioners offer inter-generational approaches for engaging with questions of death and life in a safe and supportive setting. The material guides church communities who are dealing with the death of loved ones and other situations of loss in talking together as a church family, in applying the Christian message of the resurrection in challenging situations, and in listening to each other and developing their own insights.

Seriously Messy
Making space for families to talk together about death and life
Joanna Collicutt, Lucy Moore, Martyn Payne, Victoria Slater
978 0 85746 823 9 £8.99

brfonline.org.uk

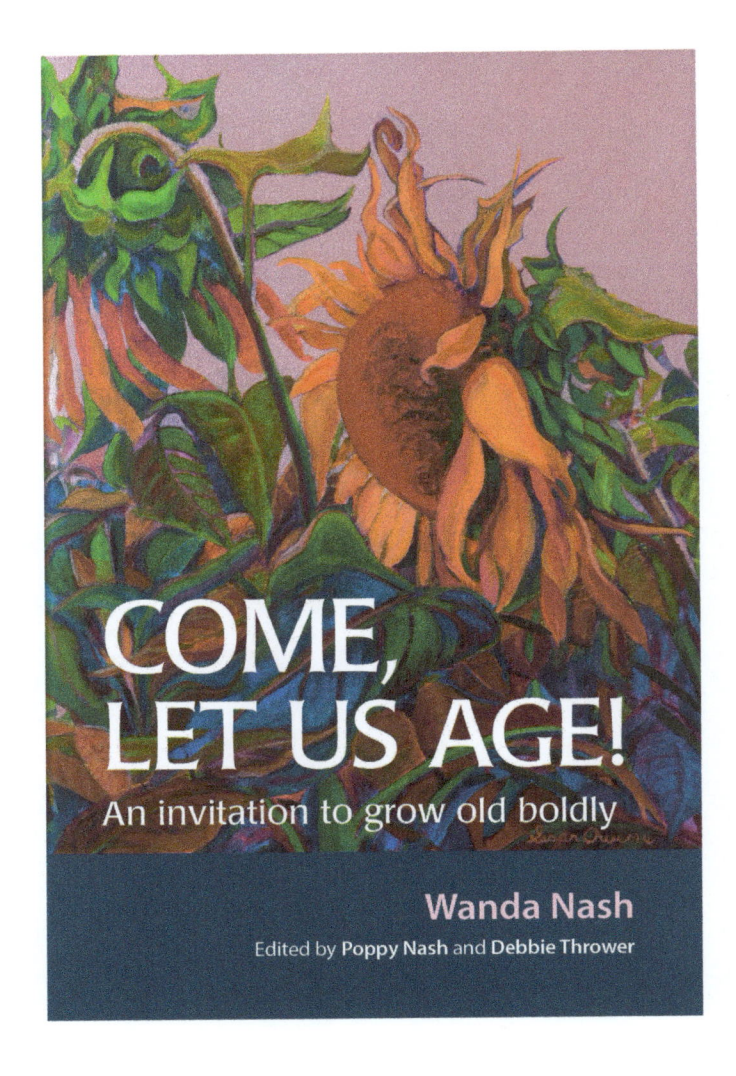

In this unique book, Wanda Nash, a well-established writer on spirituality in her late seventies, reflects on growing old with faith and a positive spirit. This compelling invitation to grow old boldly – full of her own experiences and insights – includes Wanda's reflection on her encounter later in life with terminal cancer, and her thoughts on coping with the daily challenges of living a Christian life in her illness and in ageing. Demonstrating a profound sense of the value and purposefulness of 'old age', the author's indomitable spirit is matched only by her fresh vision of the love of God in Jesus Christ.

Come, Let Us Age!
An invitation to grow old boldly
Wanda Nash
978 0 85746 558 0 £6.99

brfonline.org.uk

Grief Notes
Walking through loss
The first year after bereavement
Tony Horsfall

In *Grief Notes*, Tony Horsfall charts the first year of his grief journey since the death of his wife from cancer. Month by month he tells the unfolding story of walking with and through loss, weaving this together with biblical teaching on grief and insights gained from grief counselling. With a poignant mix of honesty and humour, Tony shares the challenges of rebuilding his life and reflects on how he has seen God meet his needs as he wrestled with grieving in a time of lockdown and pandemic.

Grief Notes
Walking through loss, the first year after bereavement
Tony Horsfall
978 1 80039 126 0 £8.99

brfonline.org.uk

Bible readings for special times

Bereavement
Jean Watson

This book of 24 undated reflections draws comfort and inspiration from the Bible and from experience for those who are going through a time of bereavement, as well as providing insight for those wanting to support others who are bereaved. Jean Watson suggests how it might feel to get through the dark days and to move, however slowly, from 'getting by' with help, to 'getting a life' in which living with loss goes alongside the gains in terms of new insights on faith and life and a greater ability to empathise with others.

Bereavement
Jean Watson
978 0 85746 326 5 £4.99

brfonline.org.uk

Bible readings for special times

Facing Death
Rachel Boulding

This book of 18 undated reflections draws comfort and encouragement from the Bible and from the author's own experience for those going through life-limiting illness and for their family and carers. With moving vulnerability and without denying the difficult reality of the situation, Rachel Boulding suggests a way to confront terminal illness with faith and hope in a loving God.

Facing Death
Rachel Boulding
978 0 85746 564 1 £3.99

brfonline.org.uk

BRF Ministries

Inspiring people of all ages to grow in Christian faith

BRF Ministries is the home of Anna Chaplaincy, Living Faith, Messy Church and Parenting for Faith

As a charity, our work would not be possible without fundraising and gifts in wills.
To find out more and to donate,
visit brf.org.uk/give or call +44 (0)1235 462305

Registered with FUNDRAISING REGULATOR